# MONEY
## on the
# TABLE
## Referrals in the Bank

*Dr. Ivan Misner and Lee Abraham*

©2011 by Ivan Misner and Lee Abraham

Cover art and layout design by Douglas Golner – www.dgmedia-design.com

Published by FAST180 Press
**www.fast180.com**

Printed in the United States of America
First Edition, First Printing: May 2011

ISBN–13 - 9780615486765
ISBN-10 – 0615486762

# Contents

# Acknowledgements

## Lee Abraham

Thank you to Dr. Misner for your contributions as co-author of this book. I am honored by the collaboration and forever appreciative of your support.

Eternal gratitude goes out to all the BNI members who shared their Givers Gain® insight and networking secrets for this book. Your success stories breathe life into the material, making it easy for others to see themselves succeed as they follow your examples. I applaud you…BRAVO!

A very special note of appreciation to my mom and dad for all that you've done throughout my life, always with my best interests at heart. I love you both! And to my good buddy Peter Lifson – the world has never known a kinder spirit and I will never find a better friend.

Most of all, thank you to my beautiful wife Marcía, for her unconditional love and support. This book has been in the works for several years. After a while, people (even those who love you the most) start to wonder what's actually going on. Days, weeks, months and years go by. They hear the keyboard clicking and see all the other work being done, but the book remains nothing more than a goal. A dream. An abstraction. *Money on the Table* is now in print and all the hard work has paid off, however, completion of this lengthy project was only possible with my wife's kind patience, understanding and encouragement. Thank you, my love, for helping transform our dreams together into reality!

— *Lee Abraham*

# Acknowledgements
## Dr. Ivan Misner

Learning and education is a two-way street. Over the years, I've gained more insight into referral marketing and word-of-mouth networking from BNI members and directors than any other source of knowledge. I'm fortunate because I see what works for different people in a wide variety of locations and am in a position to share valuable information with others. *Money on the Table* is a perfect example. My deepest appreciation to the members of BNI who have used the concepts we talk about in this book and are helping to "change the way the world does business."

— *Dr. Ivan Misner*

# Foreword

*Nathan Dominguez*
*Executive Director of BNI Arizona*

The days of print advertising and cold calling are over. In today's Internet world of Facebook and Twitter, business building has evolved from trying to sell to people who don't know you, like you, or trust you, to creating and nurturing real, mutually beneficial relationships. Whether face-to-face or online, referrals and word-of-mouth networking are clearly the present and future of wealth creation.

When I first read a draft of *Money on the Table*, I immediately knew that this book was the key to unlocking the mystery of word-of-mouth referrals for business networkers around the world.

From my vantage point, as the Executive Director of BNI Arizona and son of BNI's CEO, Norm Dominguez, I've seen lots of books and training systems on referrals and networking over the years. Let me put this into perspective: I recently turned thirty and have been around structured business networking since I was seven years old. I have seen first-hand how someone's choice of networking partners and the structure of their networking group can make or break you.

More than luck, the ability to select and cultivate mutually beneficial relationships with high-quality people in strategically important business categories is a core competency for maximum success in networking. This book is an easy-to-follow guide for building a "Power Team" of networking partners who will create an ongoing stream of referrals for your business.

Not only have Dr. Ivan Misner and Lee Abraham created the ultimate blueprint for building a Power Team, the real breakthrough of *Money on the Table* is making it easy to recognize referral opportunities we all overlook on a daily basis! Learn the "Six Key Situations" and you will be amazed at how many opportunities you've missed and how many visible and audible cues you now begin to recognize to create money-making referrals for someone you are already networking with.

The result? Give more referrals and your networking partners become increasingly motivated to reciprocate and find referrals for you.

Finally, because I have been involved in networking since I was a kid, many of the more seasoned networkers I know refer to me as a "Next Generation" networker, someone who grew up with a computer keyboard on my lap and a cell phone in my ear. In fact, for a short while back in the early days, I was actually the one man "IT" department for BNI! Here's the point: *Money on the Table* is the first book I've ever read that successfully integrates Internet strategies and networking online into a full spectrum of training on word-of-mouth referrals.

Dr. Ivan Misner is clearly regarded as the ultimate authority on business networking and referral marketing. My old friend Lee Abraham is also one of the best networkers, teachers and mentors I have ever met. My recommendation is that you don't just skim through this book and then let it wind up back on the shelf. Instead, learn this material by practicing the simple relationship-building techniques included in this book and you will see your network, your Power Team and your business grow exponentially!

— *Nathan Dominguez*

# Introduction

In 1993, I wanted to grow my real estate appraisal business in Las Vegas, Nevada, so I joined BNI, the world's largest business networking organization, to take advantage of BNI's structured system of word-of-mouth networking.

During my first few years attending BNI meetings, I began noticing some intriguing patterns as a wide variety of businesses exchanged lucrative referrals. Every time the Realtor in our group sold a house, he walked into the weekly networking meeting with a fistful of great referrals that always resulted in business for the mortgage person, insurance agent, home inspector—and myself, the real estate appraiser. Whenever the event planner landed a wedding party job, she had referrals for the caterer, photographer, florist and limousine service. For the chiropractor, a new client frequently turned into work for the massage therapist, nutritional supplement representative, a personal trainer or physical therapist.

I started calling these favorable referral circumstances "Key Situations." Over time, I categorized more than 30 Key Situations that have created a massive number of referrals for a variety of businesses in my networking group.

Then I began to look beyond the obvious referral connections among related businesses, like the Events Contact Sphere (caterer, photographer, florist) or the Real Estate group (Realtor, mortgage, insurance), to find bigger and potentially more lucrative connections between seemingly unrelated businesses.

I taped a four foot by four foot spreadsheet to my office wall and analyzed dozens of Key Situations to see how many in this wide variety of seemingly unrelated business categories could provide a product or service that would be of value to a customer or prospect in each Key Situation. In other words, could all these businesses work more closely together with referrals than they were already doing?

The results astounded me. With constant refining of the system, I ultimately was able to simplify it into six common, easy-to-recognize Key Situations that most people come in contact with regularly. As a result, I uncovered more hidden referrals among businesses that appeared to have nothing to do with each other than I'd ever imagined.

Together with Dr. Ivan Misner's unique insight and perspectives, we are sharing this powerful information with you so that you and your networking partners can benefit from what we've learned. — *Lee Abraham*

# Section I
# Power Team Toolbox

# Let's Get Started

If someone you know has given you this book, congratulations! You are already connected to a person who is an experienced referral networker with the ability to see money on the table that you've been overlooking. This book will allow you to plug into our easy-to-follow system and discover what you've been missing.

If you picked up this book on your own, without the direction of a networking partner, again: congratulations! This book was written for you. Prepare yourself for a leadership journey where you will learn not only how to generate an ongoing stream of money-making referrals, but one that will empower you to help others achieve the life of their dreams.

So what is the point of this book? Well, basically, we've written it to help you make more money. Plain and simple.

Not by creating new products or branching out into new services. Not by working longer hours, spending advertising dollars or attending more networking events. The only thing new here is a focus on something you already have: Money on the Table.

Money on the Table is an easy-to-remember phrase for networking opportunities you've been overlooking. It's also a step-by-step system to start converting those opportunities into business.

By networking around the money on the table that you have in common with other potential partners, you can create a "Power Team" of referral sources that is limited only by the size of your imagination. Let's begin with imagination.

# Chapter 1

# *More than Money*

Imagine yourself sitting at a desk, looking at several videos of two people talking. The people are different in each video. Regardless, one person is always dressed in a Superman-style superhero costume but instead of a big S on the chest, the costume is emblazoned with the letters PT.

PT stands for Power Team.

The person wearing the Superman suit is your Power Team networking partner.

Each brief video shows a different Power Team partner chatting with a random person in a different setting: a doctor's waiting room, a supermarket checkout line, an industry trade show, a local political gathering, a sporting event, the family dinner table. Always, two people are talking and one wears a PT superhero costume.

The conversations concern new babies, people moving in or out of town, weddings, real estate deals, health challenges, or making money in a terrible economy: life, death, taxes.

Watching these videos, you notice a pattern emerge. In each scene, the Power Team partner asks a question. Either: "What's the next big event coming up for you?" Or: "What's your biggest challenge at the moment?"

This is pointed key-situation dialogue: Your Power Team partner is prospecting for you.

## *Getting Married = Getting Paid*

Let's look at one possible scenario with which we're all familiar: weddings. Imagine for a moment that *regardless of what business you are in*, when a prospect talks to your Power Team partner about someone he or she knows who is getting married, you get paid.

Stay with us.

Don't wonder what weddings have to do with *you* making money if you're not a caterer, a florist, a videographer, a photographer, or even a wedding planner. That all comes later. For the moment, simply imagine getting paid from conversations involving people who are getting married.

Let's go back to you sitting at your computer. Now imagine the computer keyboard. In the upper right corner is a new key you have never seen before! Dark green like the color of money and the size of a silver dollar, it is labeled *"Getting Married."*

Imagine how great it would be if you could make money by clicking on the green Getting Married key every time the topic of conversation on the computer screen turned to someone getting married. That's it! As soon as the prospect who is talking to your Power Team partner says that he, or someone he knows, is getting married, the Getting Married tag pops up, you click on the screen and *ka-ching*—you get paid!

## Pick Your Team

Here's a bonus: Before the networking scenes even begin to flash across the screen, you get to select ten Power Team partners from different business categories and the key situations you get paid for. You can select from an enormous list of different business and life-event categories that are tied together.

Let's return to getting paid for the wedding scenario conversations. Of course, you will get paid more often by increasing the number of conversations about weddings, so it makes sense to select an event planner, a jeweler, a caterer, a florist, and a photographer: businesses that thrive on weddings.

## Givers Gain®

So where does getting paid fit in? Specifically, how do you get paid when your Power Team talks to people involved in a wedding? Especially if weddings have nothing to do with your current business (or so it appears.)

The answer: *You create business for your networking partners who offer a product or service that directly benefits someone getting married or planning a wedding.* In return, your networking partner goes the extra mile to create business for you.

The term Givers Gain® is a version of "what goes around comes around". Help others first and they will help you in return.[1]

---

1    *I coined the term, which uses two words to articulate a powerful, universally appealing philosophy that can take years, or even decades to master – Dr. Ivan Misner*

## Why Weddings?

Good question. Weddings are the low-hanging fruit of networking creating demand for the products and services of a wide cross-section of industry groups. Just think about all the planning and different arrangements needed to make the wedding happen.

Start with the jeweler, where the husband-to-be (or increasingly, the couple) chooses the engagement ring. Even before he pops the question, the prospective groom is likely to have visited a florist for a bouquet of flowers and reserved a table at a romantic restaurant to propose. So months ahead of that walk down the aisle, money has already been placed on the table.

When the bride-to-be gets involved, the wheels of commerce spin faster as an event planner, caterer, photographer, printer, travel agent, and limousine service will all generate business from the upcoming wedding ceremony, reception and honeymoon.

Many of the businesses involved at this point will already be connected professionally from working together on other weddings and events. In some cases, they will actually recommend the services of one or two of the other vendors based on the client's needs. Why give the referral? Because they know the client will be happy with the results, which in turn makes them look good and leads to further referrals down the line.

These businesses are all in what networkers refer to as a Contact Sphere, and these businesses are all in the same Contact Sphere. In other words, they are related, non-competing, complementary and symbiotic businesses. Let's call this the Events Contact Sphere.

These businesses may have links to each other on their websites. Or business-card displays at each other's offices or stores. Good stuff, but more is possible. Working together in an organized, structured way, this group of businesses has the potential to systematically increase everyone's business with more qualified referrals passed back and forth again and again.

Remember: the more businesses in your Power Team that work for the same client and also understand how to create business for each other, the greater good for all.

## Honeymoons, Newlyweds and Planning for the Future

Back to the happy couple. As they plan to merge their lives, various other businesses enter the field. It expands past the one-time event of the wedding (at least that's the hope!) and creates even more referrals. This is where the often overlooked Money on the Table concept really becomes apparent.

Handling day-to-day details is part of this. Simple acts such as switching cell phone usage to a family plan, hiring a cleaning service or pet sitter, buying new art or furniture as a couple, maybe selling a home, or buying a new home together, are all examples of opportunities that can lead to more referrals.

There's also planning for the future. Smart, young couples start investing today for retirement or a college fund. They also spend money on life and disability insurance or hire a lawyer for a Will or a Trust.

We are now looking at a much more varied group of businesses than those who may already know each other from working together at weddings. Now we are expanding your awareness of where to find money on the table for your Power Team with a few examples of referral opportunities that are routinely overlooked.

True, the interior designer and the furniture salesperson might already know and refer clients to each other. After all, they are both part of another Contact Sphere, this one Property Services. Another Contact Sphere that is made up of the attorney, the financial planner and insurance agent is the Real Estate/Finance Contact Sphere. The pet service and personal chef businesses are part of the Personal Services Contact Sphere. And so on.

All of the businesses inside these various groups have a good chance of knowing each other because of the obvious and frequent overlap they have in working for the same type of client.

*Our goal is that all of the businesses in your network expand their awareness beyond their own Contact Sphere to recognize a prospect's full spectrum of needs and how other Contact Spheres and industry groups can serve them.* In other words, we want you to easily recognize money on the table for any industry and any business category in your network.

## Power Team

Imagine what would happen if the first business person involved in this sequence of business activity, the jeweler, took a moment with every wedding ring customer to say: "Now that we've finished our business and you are happy with these beautiful rings, I would like to give you this brochure with information about a group of businesses I work with whenever possible."

"These people are great at what they do," the jeweler adds. "*I know them personally and use their products and services myself.* They might have products or services that you will need for your wedding, and maybe some things you haven't thought about yet for married life. In any case, here's the list. Let me know if I can help you with more information on any of these businesses."

## Last Becomes First

In the earlier example about future planning, the last wedding-related referral was the lawyer who handles Wills or Trusts. Perhaps the lawyer's client—a man who is to be married—wants a Will drawn up to protect his fiancée in the event something happens to him before their wedding several months away.

The lawyer's Power Team radar alerts him to the business potential in his client's wedding.

After completing the Will for his client, the lawyer might say, "Now that we've finished our business and you've arranged this Will to protect your fiancée— it's obvious you like to think ahead and plan for contingencies. So let me give you this flyer with information about a group of businesses I work with whenever possible."

Not every business within the group may be applicable. It's likely that the lawyer's client has already purchased the wedding rings but he may not have hired a photographer, booked a honeymoon, looked into a cell phone "family plan" or met with a Realtor to sell or buy a home. Nevertheless, the lawyer is looking to broaden his client's awareness of the products and services offered by his Power Team and, as a result, expand his referral business.

## Show Me the Money

We've all heard the saying, "It takes money to make money." We believe that cliché is, in fact, only partially true.

Sure, with enough cash, you can pay as many people or buy as many ads as it takes to build sales volume. But such expense is risky. Too often, businesses spend more on marketing and advertising than they get back in increased sales.

Now, every business needs a sales force. We all benefit from people who keep their eyes and ears open on a daily basis, eagerly searching for opportunities to refer business our way. And yes, the sales force needs to be motivated.

Obviously, money is the most common motivator but networking can be more efficient and effective.

With training and strategic planning, a Power Team of people who have made a mutual commitment to build each other's businesses will become your most active networking partners and in many ways, your best salespeople.

Make no mistake, word-of-mouth networking is the most cost-effective and powerful way to build your business.

Time now for a reality check: Sure, we all love the idea of other people sending us business, but is it realistic? We know what's in it for *you*. But how about the other people? Are they motivated to help you? ***Do your networking partners care enough about your business to keep your interests top-of-mind?***

## Who Cares?

Realistically, there are only a few basic ways of motivating people to help build your business. Basically, it comes down to relationships and rewards.

Some folks, usually friends or family, will simply want to help because they like you and want you to do well. These people will be motivated by the relationship itself.

But in most other cases the long term motivation to build your business is not based primarily on whether or not the other person likes you. Business partnerships, including referral relationships, almost always include some form of mutual reward, typically in the form of social or financial gain. Both you and your networking partner have something to gain, and you are both eager to help each other achieve it.

Some people are motivated by the potential for business referrals you can send, while others are motivated by the prestige and opportunities created by having a relationship with you. Regardless of the underlying motivation behind them, relationships can take time to prove profitable in a substantial way, but that doesn't mean they aren't worth cultivating. Ultimately, strong relationships will steer back to opportunities because of the nature of networking itself and of the endless variety of products and services to which it can lead.

We firmly believe that most relationships will probably prove rewarding in the long term, even in cases where you don't receive referrals in return. There are a few super successful people to whom we send referrals who've never reciprocated with a referral back. We're motivated to continue helping them in any way we can simply because they will work with people we refer to them. That makes us look good, because it's very difficult for the average person to start a working relationship with these very successful, very busy people.

If we refer someone, it opens a door that might never have otherwise opened. The new person that we are referring to our very busy friends or associates is the one who now goes out of his way to reciprocate. That's our motivation; helping our networking partners achieve their goals. And, of course, in one form or another, it winds up coming back in some way.

## Create Networking Value with Money on the Table

Think of your Power Team as your sales force. And while you're at it, think big. Think of your Power Team as an elite, highly paid, highly motivated sales force of people who like you, trust you, and are eagerly seeking opportunities to create referrals for you and your business.

Okay, fine. Let's back up for a moment and focus on the "highly paid" piece of the puzzle.

*Where's all the money coming from to pay these people? Good news: you pay them with money on the table by systematically directing other peoples' purchase dollars to their products and services.*

Let's beat a dead horse here: create strong, money-making referrals for your networking partners and in turn, they will send paying customers to you!

Perhaps you are already giving referrals. This book will show you how to give more and better quality referrals while generating greater money-making referrals for yourself.

How?

By helping you recognize six common, everyday situations that present a wealth of opportunities to systematically build the businesses of your hand-selected Power Team.

**This book will also teach you how to train your networking partners to create business for you.**

## Ivan's Perspective
### *"Evolving Sphere—The Power Team Definition"*

"The term "Power Team" is sort of an organic phrase that sprouted from the notion of a "Contact Sphere." Everyone pretty much understood the concept of symbiotic professions that aren't competing with each other and there was a need in BNI to further differentiate between a potential networking partner and someone you are currently networking with.

I had many conversations with people who were telling me, "I have 50 percent of my Contact Sphere represented in this room right now and these are the people who have really made a commitment to help build each other's

*business." The term "Power Team" came up as a subset of*
*Contact Sphere to give a name to the group of people who*
*are the most active networkers.*

*I was really taught this term by BNI members who needed*
*to differentiate between the two concepts."*

*– Dr. Ivan Misner*

## The Wedding Power Team

Let's circle back to weddings once more. These functions create a huge opportunity to *give* referrals, regardless of the business you are in. You just need to know how the different people and businesses on your Power Team can provide a valuable product or service to the "Getting Married" targeted prospect.

Make the same sort of connections for all Six Key Situations in this book and your money on the table will become referrals in the bank.

### Ivan's Perspective
#### "BNI's First Power Team: Weddings"

"*I was visiting BNI groups on the East Coast of the United States many years ago and I had an opportunity to drop into a photographer's studio who was a member of the organization. I noticed that he had this great display of brochures and materials for several other members who were all in the same Contact Sphere: "Weddings." I spoke to him about the display and he explained that when he got a new wedding client, he always referred them to the florist, travel agent, and jeweler who were in the group with him. He said that this "Power Team" of people working in the wedding industry generated a lot of business for each other. I was very impressed.*

*Later that day, we dropped into the florist's shop who was also a member of that group. I noticed that she too had a display of all her Power Team's materials (including the photographer I visited earlier that day). When I spoke to her she laughed and said, "Yes, when someone comes in for a wedding we all highly recommend each other." She said,*

> *"We call ourselves the 'wedding mafia.' When people come in, we don't let them out until we show them our Power Team's materials!"*
>
> *This group of people passed more referrals to each other than any other group of people. They absolutely attributed it to the Power Team they formed.*
>
> *By the way, sometimes people get upset with the use of the term "mafia" (political correctness gone amok!) For the record, the origin of the term actually means "any small powerful or influential group in an organization or field." That certainly fits with this group."*
>
> *– Dr. Ivan Misner*

## Six Key Situations

After decades of analyzing how networking groups are structured, we have found that the vast majority of business referrals can be categorized into six primary Key Situations:

- Business Builder
- Getting Healthy
- Getting Married
- Relocation
- New Baby
- Real Estate (this includes: Buy / Sell / New Construction / Remodeling / Repairs / Maintenance)

This book will help you understand the dynamics of turning each Key Situation into money-making referrals for your Power Team's products and services. The more referrals you create for others, the more you will receive in return, based on the Key Situations you've trained your Power Team to recognize for you.

## Chapter 2

# *How Much Money Was Left on the Table?*

Before we dig into the mechanics of the Money on the Table system, let's take a look at hundreds of thousands of dollars in commonly overlooked referral opportunities that are too often left on the table waiting to be claimed.

The following six fictional stories paint a picture rather than explain a process. So read on, and use these stories to gain awareness and insight into the instances in your business where you are leaving money on the table.

## *A Wedding Story*

Mary noticed her client's sparkling new engagement ring immediately. Mary had been pet-sitting for this well-to-do client in her beautiful home for over a year, and her heart leapt at the sight of the huge diamond and thick gold band.

"Wow!" she said. "That is absolutely the most beautiful ring I have ever seen. When's the wedding?"

The client smiled and said, "It's coming up quick. We've set the date for early summer, and as a matter of fact, I've already started making arrangements for the ceremony and reception. But let me tell you," she added, with a note of concern, "It's turning into a real challenge. I've been talking to wedding planners all week, but haven't found one yet I really like. I'm getting a bit frustrated."

Mary, alert to referrals, saw her opening. "I can help. You must meet my friend Arnold. He's a simply fabulous wedding planner. I just joined a business networking group he also belongs to, and I already know at least a dozen people who have worked with him and they all adore him. In fact, can I have Arnold give you a call so you can decide for yourself if you would like to work with him?"

The client, thrilled with Mary's testimonial, agreed to have Arnold call her, and marveled at her luck. It had never occurred to her to ask her pet sitter for help in finding a wedding planner.

Mary was also happy with the unexpected turn of events that arose from her noticing that incredible diamond ring, and asking the pertinent question that led to the opportunity to create the referral. In other words, she never would have seen Arnold's money on the table—thousands of dollars worth of business with his name on it.

But as good as she felt from that referral, Mary realized later that she saw only a fraction of all the money on the table that this wedding could generate for the many different people in her business networking group.

For his part, Arnold, a seasoned networker and well-established event planner, handled all the details to create the client's dream wedding. In the process, he also created work for the caterer, photographer, florist, gift basket maker and the owner of the limousine service—thousands of dollars in business, this time for several businesses.

Those referrals came easily and, in fact, automatically, because those products and services dealt directly with Arnold's role in planning the wedding. "Mary, our fabulous pet sitter, set 'em up, and I knocked 'em down," Arnold boasted to his networking group's Thursday morning meeting. "I just told the client how great you all are and wrote your names into the contract as my vendors!"

Arnold took the initiative created by Mary's money-making referral and turned it into even more business for a number of the networking group's members.

Of course, creating happy, satisfied customers is Arnold's number-one priority. Experience taught him that a great team of people he trusts to provide products and services needed for every wedding event is critical to the success of his business. And if Arnold could help his friends make money in the process, even better!

Plus, let's face it: networking is fun. Handing out a bunch of done-deal referrals at a networking meeting is a blast! Lots of laughter, good cheer and even the occasional standing ovation tend to lift the energy in the meeting room when someone creates business for several of the members at the same time.

But there was one question that Arnold didn't ask his client, a question that would have created ten times more business for a much wider assortment of his networking partners. If he'd known that he'd left so much money on the table, the boisterous bantering and high-five glad-handing at his Thursday morning meeting would have evaporated.

The question he didn't ask was this:

*"What other sort of day-to-day challenges are you trying to keep up with?"*

Do you have any idea how much money Arnold left on the table by not asking this simple but powerful question?

Here's what Arnold should have done:

After Arnold and the client reached an agreement on the wedding plans and signed the contract, he should have taken his business card organizer out from his briefcase, placed it on the table and said to his client, "Now that you have hired me to handle the details of your wedding, you can focus on the rest of your life. What other sort of day-to-day challenges are you trying to keep up with? I do a lot of networking with some really amazing people and I may know the right person to help."

Nothing pushy, nothing out of sorts—simply one person offering to help another—which is the perfect situation to generate referrals.

---

*Here are some examples of the money Arnold left on the table:*

The bride and groom had already decided to sell their respective houses and build a new custom home together, something they were going to begin working on after their wedding plans were underway.

The couple's real estate activity would have been a terrific referral for his networking group's:

- **Realtor** – would have had the opportunity to earn a commission as a listing agent on the couple's two current homes as well as representing them on the purchase of the vacant lot for construction of their new custom home.

- **Interior Designer** – could have been hired to create the new home's décor as well as the selection and purchase of finish materials, furniture and accessories.

- **House, Carpet, and Window Cleaners** – all three types of cleaning services could have been brought in to make both homes spotless before being listed for sale as well as the new home prior to moving in.

- **Architect** – could have been hired to draw up the blueprints for their new custom home.

- **General Contractor** – could have been retained to build the couple's custom home, a relatively large contract, likely the biggest sum of money left on the table by failing to uncover this referral opportunity.

- **Mortgage Officer** – construction of a new custom home typically requires a special "construction loan" which converts into a home mortgage after the home is complete. Too bad the mortgage officer never got a chance to earn the money on the table that some other mortgage officer deposited in the bank.

> *Can you think of more referral opportunities? How about YOUR business, can you see any money on the table?*

If Arnold knew about the client's back pain from her injury while working on her landscaping, he could have referred her to his networking group's:

- **Chiropractor** – would have been able to possibly provide immediate relief from the back pain and perhaps develop into an ongoing program of care.

- **Massage Therapist** – very similar to the opportunity overlooked for the chiropractor, the massage therapist could have provided relief from the client's discomfort and developed into an ongoing relationship and stream of money on the table, as well as an ongoing opportunity to uncover additional referrals to the group.

- **Landscaper** – although the landscaper could have easily come to mind as a potential referral based on the client's real estate activity, this referral could have also been triggered by learning of the client's back injury while doing her own landscaping. The same logic applies to the cleaning businesses.

> *Can you think of more referral opportunities? How about YOUR business – can you see any money on the table?*

Had Arnold known about his client's inexperience with financial planning, he could have created a flurry of business by referring her to the group's:

- **Accountant** – could have helped them take advantage of

various tax planning strategies for married couples and other money management details.

- **Investment Advisor** – could have been a valuable resource providing a financial plan to begin saving and investing for retirement and possible college fund if the couple  plans to have children.

- **Attorney** – imagine the peace of mind the attorney could have offered with a Will or a Trust to protect the other spouse in the event of a tragedy.

- **Insurance** – in addition to the attorney, the insurance agent could have helped the couple protect themselves against unforeseen tragedy with a complete package of life, health and disability insurance.

The exact amount of money left on the table is impossible to calculate. However, it is safe to say that Mary and Arnold's networking group could have easily gained a substantial amount of business *by asking a few more simple questions* that we call "*Trigger Questions*" (we'll train you on them a bit later in this book).

## A Getting Healthy Story

Flashing red lights reflected in the twisted metal of the crashed sports car. A puddle of transmission fluid formed beside the mangled wreck and broken glass was everywhere, sparkling brightly in the sunlight against the road's black asphalt. It was a chilling scene.

Emergency vehicles had just arrived and paramedics found both driver and passenger, two young businessmen in their mid 30's, conscious but dazed and motionless inside the vehicle.

Driving home from an afternoon of golf, Steve Jagger, a successful general contractor and avid sportsman, suddenly swerved to avoid another car that abruptly turned into his lane without looking. He didn't swerve in time. The two cars collided, spun out of control, and he slammed into a stand of trees just a few yards from the side of the road. Airbags deployed and after regaining a little composure, Rob Smith, Steve's passenger and friend, dialed 911 for help.

Both men were held at the hospital overnight for observation. Rob was released the next morning with a sore body and a bottle of pain meds. Steve wasn't so lucky. Suffering a concussion, several broken ribs, and an assortment of other injuries, he would remain in the hospital for at least a week. It would be a lot longer before Steve returned to his normal routine as a general contractor. There was plenty of rehab to be done before he was back on the construction site.

Although stiff and still a bit bleary, Rob was back working at his auto body repair shop the next day. Eerily, Steve's sports car, with its badly damaged front end and shattered windshield, was there waiting for him. Rob got goose bumps thinking about how lucky he was to be alive and relatively unharmed from the accident.

His thoughts turned quickly to Steve. Rob called home and asked his wife, Jane, to check with the hospital for an update. It was Jane who originally introduced the two golfing buddies. Jane met Steve when she joined a local networking group to grow the auto body repair business. At the time, Steve was president of the group and ran its weekly meetings.

"It'll be a while before you two go golfing again," Jane said later. "Steve will be home in four or five days and he's going to be out of commission for at least the first month of his recovery, maybe longer."

"Ouch!" Rob said. "As a single guy with a lot going on, including running a business, this is really going to cause some serious problems for Steve. I wonder if there's anyone in your business networking group who might step up and lend him a hand?"

"Actually, several people could really make Steve's life a lot easier," Jane agreed. "I'm sure we can make some good things happen."

Good things did happen. At her networking meeting the next morning, Jane told the group about the accident and Steve's need for help while recovering. The response was overwhelming. During the three years he had been a member of this group, Steve had created business for almost everyone involved. The Realtor, the mortgage expert, the insurance agent and the interior designer had been particularly fortunate to receive a huge volume of money-making referrals from their good buddy Steve, the general contractor. Even the personal chef and florist, who rarely got a referral from Steve, had benefited from his leadership, in part due to Steve's role in recruiting the group's new caterer, a great source of business for both.

"The florist has already sent a nice flower arrangement to brighten up Steve's room at the hospital," Jane told Rob later. "The cleaning service and landscaper volunteered to take care of his house for as long as he needs them. Same with the pet sitter for dog walks. The Realtor said he would cover costs for the personal chef to bring Steve hot, ready-to-eat, home-cooked meals. And the massage therapist, chiropractor and personal trainer all offered their services at no charge whenever Steve was ready."

"This whole thing really got me thinking," Jane added. "We were extremely lucky that you didn't wind up in the same condition as Steve, so I took action and passed a referral for you and me to meet with our insurance agent. Now is the time for us to stop risking our security and get the life and disability coverage we've been putting off."

Rob nodded. "You know, I just had a great idea," he said. "We get wrecked vehicles in here every day of the week, and every one of those cars is owned by somebody who was in an accident and might benefit from a product or service of someone in the networking group. I'm going to create a flyer we can give to our customers that briefly explains how people in the network can help."

"We'll also put a business card display in our lobby area," he went on, "and maybe we could even put together a short video to post on YouTube and email it to our customers who physically can't come down to the shop!"

The flyers, business card display and YouTube video proved to be outstandingly effective marketing tools. Almost every customer contacted and did business with at least one, and in some cases several of the team's networking partners.

Here are a few examples of money on the table Jane and Rob could find for their networking partners by systematically making their network visible to all of their customers.

People recovering from injury or illness often need help performing routine daily tasks around the house which puts money on the table for a variety of business categories in the Personal Services and Property Services Contact Spheres in Jane's networking group:

- **Errand/Delivery Service** – can be a valuable resource, not only to help with groceries, mail and other errands, but also for running around performing similar activities for an injured person's business.

- **Personal Chef** – surprisingly affordable solution for people recovering from illness or injury. Healthy home-cooked meals in the case of the example, may have also continued to be of interest to Steve after his recovery, as a busy single man who likely doesn't do a lot of cooking for himself.

- **Pet Service** – dog walks, feeding and potty breaks are three simple, yet critical daily responsibilities that the prospect may not be able to perform. Again, in our example, as a busy, single man Steve may become a regular client if he is also a pet owner.

- **Landscaping** – people in recovery who own property have an additional set of responsibilities that include property maintenance and landscaping. Another service that Steve may be happy to pay for even after fully recovered. Why? So he can spend more time on his business.

- **Cleaning** – a parallel product and service to the landscaper, ongoing chores inside the home can be even more essential in cases of recovery from illness. The reason? The connection between cleanliness and overcoming health challenges.

*Can you think of more referral opportunities? How about YOUR business, can you see any money on the table?*

Physical recovery from injury or illness is a team effort. Expertise from trusted health and wellness professionals for help with proper nutrition and diet, as well as several other members of the group who can provide body work, exercise, and overall mental health, could all be of service during the recovery.

- **Nutritionist** – recovery from illness or injury is often the wake-up-call people need to become more proactive in their own health. A referral to a nutritionist not only uncovers money on the table immediately, it is common for nutritional products to be delivered on an automatic, monthly auto-shipment – creating an ongoing stream of income for the nutritionist.

- **Personal Trainer** – another key to recovery, the more you know about your personal trainer's education and experience the more compelling referrals you'll be able to give.

- **Chiropractor** – again, the more actual experience you have with the chiropractor and the greater your knowledge of your chiropractor's background and success stories you can retell, the more successful you will be as a Bragging Buddy.

- **Massage Therapist** – very similar to the chiropractor, it is easy to see how these two business professions, along with the nutritionist and personal trainer can create a dynamite Power Team by systematically making their network visible to every customer.

- **Life Coach** – not as obvious of a referral opportunity as some of the other health and wellness business categories. A qualified and effective life coach can offer significant value to a person in recovery. Likewise, life coaches are always working with people in life's transitions which, in turn, enables creation of an ongoing stream of referral opportunities for the other members of the Power Team.

---

Nothing shocks someone into behavior modification like a life-threatening injury or serious illness and it's not only the person in recovery who makes changes. Many times, ***through a loved one's tragic experience, people see themselves as vulnerable to mortality for the first time and take action by purchasing insurance, starting an investment plan, and making a Will or a Trust to protect their family.*** Same idea with purchasing a home security and fire alarm system or performing needed maintenance to a vehicle.

- **Attorney, Financial Planner and Life and Disability Insurance** are the "big three" business categories from the Financial Services Contact Sphere that almost always have money on the table in recovery situations. More on this later.

- **Home Security and Fire Alarm** – in addition to their

standard security and safety products including "Medical Alert" devices, intercoms and videocams to enable two-way communications from the recovery bedroom to other rooms inside the home, are often a terrific value in these situations.

- **Automobile Maintenance** – particularly in cases of recovery from injury in an auto accident, the more you know about your auto mechanic's skill and honesty the stronger the referrals you will be able to give.

---

*Can you think of more referral opportunities? How about YOUR business, can you see any money on the table?*

---

Some Getting Healthy Key Situations, particularly cases of permanent or long-term disability, require modifications to the layout or other features of a home. Remodeling a kitchen or bathroom, purchasing medically necessary bedding and other ergonomic furniture, as well as installation of water purification and air filtration systems, are products and services often needed by people homebound with a physical disability or chronic illness.

- **Contractor** – kitchen and bathroom alterations to accommodate reduced mobility are frequent needs, and lucrative streams of referrals.

- **Water and Air Filtration** – recovery from serious injury is impacted by the quality of the air being breathed and the water being consumed, as well as absorbed into the body through bathing and showering. Your familiarity with the benefits of these products and systems as well as the people in your group who offer them, the greater value you will be to the person recovering their health and the more quality referrals you will create for your Power Team.

---

*Can you think of more referral opportunities? How about YOUR business, can you see any money on the table?*

---

Although it is unlikely a customer would need the product or service of every business in the network, there are large sums of money on the table every time a smashed vehicle is brought into the repair shop.

Both Jane and Rob are now determined to find out if any of that money has their networking partners' names on it.

# A Business-Builder Story

Joe loved his new website.

Even on the small screen of his well-traveled laptop, the close-up photo of Joe's smiling face on the site's splash page lit up the room. It showed him onstage and playing guitar, with the effortless oh-so-cool body language of a true guitar master. This was a powerful, compelling visual image. Students who want guitar lessons look for precisely that "music guru" persona when they search online.

Years ago, when Joe was in a rock band, he went on tour for months at a time traveling from town to town in a van with four other guys. "Sleeping in low budget motels or on the floor of a stinky van is fine when you're young," Joe told Kay, his website designer. "Driving nonstop in that van for so many hours and sleeping like a hobo for months at a time took a toll on my back and neck. But now I'm too old and too fat for that lifestyle. I barely have enough energy for five or six hours a day sitting in a chair and teaching guitar. Plus, with all the things I need to do around the house with our kids and our dog, I just can't pick up and travel as easily as I used to, so I'm grateful I can sell my music through the terrific website you've created for me!"

Kay, with a husband, two children and a house to maintain, empathized. "I can't help you with your aching back and neck," she said, "but I do think we've got one rockin' website here for you!"

"Joe's Music Lessons" website was indeed awesome.

Joe had met Kay through a student of his, an accountant who, at age 55, decided to take up his lifelong dream of playing guitar. During one of the accountant's lessons, Joe mentioned to him a brand new guitar-lesson DVD he was trying to sell for some extra money. The accountant told Joe about Kay, who was in his business networking group, and about her specialty of creating websites that sell products. He asked Joe if it would be okay to give Kay his number. That was the beginning of a great business relationship. Kay's web design and search engine optimization worked well and the website took off.

"Yes, it's true that I am a great guitar teacher, good looking, and entertaining, as well," Joe said with a laugh. "But the only reason I'm selling so many DVDs is your expertise in getting it out to the consumers on the Internet. I've got a new DVD coming out in a few weeks, and my income has almost doubled from all the DVD sales on the website. I can't thank you enough!"

Sure, both Joe and Kay are happy campers. And why not? Making money will put a smile on anyone's face.

But in this case, ignorance was bliss.

Imagine how much happier Kay and Joe would be, as well as the accountant and Kay's other networking partners, if she had seen all the money on the table with her Power Team partners' names on it.

It's hard to tell how much money Kay left on the table by missing several easy-to-recognize referral opportunities, but we can make some fairly reasonable guesses.

Here are some ideas:

With Joe making more money, he could benefit from expert tax and investment planning, giving him more cash flow for marketing and promotion. In addition to creating a local product launch event for his new DVD, Joe could benefit from a business coach to hone his business and networking skills, as well as promote more products (maybe guitar picks and tuners with his name and logo), a customer appreciation event and follow-up system (greeting cards and gift baskets) to build his personal brand and customer loyalty.

That would have been a terrific opportunity for several people in Kay's networking group:

- **Accountant** – tax planning pays off for business builders with a rising income. More good news: You do not need to know the details of how the accountant works their magic. You do, however, need to be able to retell a success story or two and have a compelling testimonial for the accountant's skill and authentic interest in the client's best interest.

- **Attorney** – as the dollars go up the exposure to liability and lawsuits over contract agreements or customer satisfaction increases as well. An attorney who specializes in business law is a valuable resource you can connect to the rising business stars you encounter in your daily business life.

- **Financial Planner** – business builders are often so focused on building their business that opportunities to maximize financial gain through expert planning will fall through the cracks, along with the money on the table for the financial planner on your Power Team.

- **Event Planner** – a creative approach to generating referrals for your event planner is to recognize the opportunity to suggest a product launch event, open house, media day, public workshop or other creative business building idea related to hosting an event to promote the business.

- **Caterer** – in tandem with the event planner, the caterer is one of many business categories from the Events Contact Sphere that can provide significant value to a business building event. More on this later in the book.

- **Business Trainer** – business builders are almost always good at producing and delivering their product or service, however they are rarely skilled at business itself. Smart business builders recognize that rather than fly by the seat of their pants, there is value in learning from a business trainer, coach or consultant who can guide a more efficient and effective allocation of time, energy and resources. Like most of the business categories on your Power Team, you don't need to know all the details of how they do what they do, you just need success stories to retell and a sincere belief that your business trainer can help them.

- **Promotional Products** – more than just pens and coffee mugs, a creative and knowledgeable promotional products salesperson can help a business builder make their brand more visible and create more sales. The more top-of-mind your promotional products salesperson is for you, the more you will see money on the table for them when you talk to a business builder.

---

If Kay had been *listening more intently, she would have asked a few questions when Joe complained about his physical ailments.* From Joe's description of his bad neck and back, to his being overweight, out-of-shape and having no energy, Kay overlooked several red flags for making referrals:

- **Nutritionist** – more energy and fewer sick days means more productivity and more business. Music to the ears of the business builder and a solid ka-ching to the ears of your Power Team. Can you sing the praises of your nutritionist?

- **Personal Trainer** – visual and audio cues from people who would benefit from weight loss are everywhere. Your comfort level in your networking partner's ability to make you look good is critical in your willingness and enthusiasm to venture conversation into this potentially uncomfortable topic. From the perspective of the personal trainer, the goal is to show your Power Team why you are great at helping people get into shape and how to easily recognize prospects who would likely benefit from your service.

- **Chiropractor** – bad backs and other ailments from long-term sitting, standing or other day-to-day repetitive physical activities are common for business builders. The more you know about the chiropractor's success stories and quality of care, the more effective Bragging Buddy you will be.

- **Massage Therapist** – in addition to relieving physical stress which in turns creates more energy and focus for the business builder, the massage therapist can also provide "in office" chair massage for the staff or gift certificates as thank-you gifts for the business builder's clients, staff and vendors.

- **Ergonomic Furniture Sales** – another often overlooked, yet well-connected business category for powerful networking opportunities with business builders, ergonomic furniture products offer increased performance from longer endurance on jobs that require long-term sitting, and also beds for better sleep at night which result in more energy at work the next day. If you don't currently have a furniture sales expert in your Power Team, go find one. If you are one: build a Power Team and systematically make it visible. You will be amazed at the results!

---

With Joe's business growing, he would benefit from paying other people to do a variety of simple tasks for him, so he could have more time to build his business. Here are a few examples of referral opportunities for businesses in the Property Services and Personal Services Contact Spheres.

- **Cleaning Service** – cleaning both the home and office are possible ongoing services and referrals for all types of cleaning services including general cleaning, carpet, windows and laundry.

- **Personal Chef** – surprisingly affordable, a valuable time saver and, in fact, a well-deserved reward for the business builder.

- **Pet Sitter** – business builders with pets are a strong targeted prospect for pet sitters. To consistently receive more business builder referrals, pet sitters must achieve top-of-mind awareness with their networking partners to recognize visual and audio cues that the business builder is a pet owner **and** systematically make the pet sitter's value visible to the business builder with a business card organizer, directory or website.

- **Landscaper** – unless gardening is viewed as an enjoyable pastime and opportunity to decompress and relax from the rigors of building a business, landscape maintenance is a "no brainer" referral for the busy business builder who owns a home or business property.

> **Can you think of more referral opportunities? How about YOUR business – can you see any money on the table?**

In the end, regardless of the actual figure, the amount of money left on the table is way too high. Particularly when it could have easily been turned into money-making referrals for Kay's networking group, if only she'd been alert enough to ask a few more questions.

# A New Baby Story

Jack crawled out from under the desk, dusted himself off, and rebooted the computer one more time. Within seconds, the monitor prompted him for an ID and password. His fingers responded in a blur, and everything seemed to be working fine. The computer network of Thompson's Plumbing was back online and Jack made his way to the front office to let the owner know.

Before entering the office, Jack overheard the owner, Ernie Thompson, talking on the telephone with his wife. "Honey, I know you're feeling tired and run down," he said affectionately. "I think it's time we listen to the doctor's advice and get both you and the baby on some good prenatal vitamins. It's still very early in your pregnancy, but you are starting to the pay the price of procrastinating and that can't be good for the baby or for you."

Mr. Thompson looked up and saw Jack outside the office door. Telling his wife he'd call her back, he placed the receiver down and asked Jack to come into the office.

"Just a bad router, Mr. Thompson," Jack said. "Replaced it with a new one and you're good to go. I just need to clean up my mess before I leave."

Ernie Thompson liked working with Jack. Not only was he a computer whiz, but very reliable and fairly priced. Plus, Jack had connections. The promotional products lady Jack recommended the year before had come up with some great ideas to increase local recognition of the Thompson Plumbing brand. The result: big service and maintenance contracts for two large apartment complexes in the area. Based on past performance, if Jack gave a strong recommendation, Mr. Thompson would take it.

"I inadvertently overheard you on the phone with your wife," Jack said. "If it's not too forward, I want to let you know about some great nutritional supplements, including a prenatal vitamin, from my friend Dave that might help her. Dave's been in the nutrition business for a long time and only sells the highest quality products. Well, he told the group today at our networking meeting about several case studies proving the safety and effectiveness of these vitamins for healthy moms and babies. He really made me a believer! Would it be okay if I have Dave give you a call to talk about his products?"

Thompson agreed. "Any help I can get is much appreciated. My wife really is having a tough time, lots of back pain and discomfort. She's not sleeping well and I'm hoping these vitamins will make a difference."

"I'm sure they will," said Jack. "One of the other things I learned today was how closely Dave works with both the chiropractor and massage therapist in my networking group. As it turns out, they are both specially trained in prenatal body work and have a lot of success in helping women who are having difficulties during pregnancy."

"Well, have them call me, too," said Thompson with a chuckle. "Let's get your whole group involved."

Jack was tickled with his good luck. Being in the right place at the right time gave him the opportunity to create three referrals for his networking partners! But had Jack taken literally Thompson's comment to get his whole group involved, he would have used one simple technique to uncover a big stack of money on the table waiting to be claimed for his networking partners.

Here's a technique we explain later in the book:

After sharing a laugh with Mr. Thompson, Jack could have said, "Here's my business organizer with cards from all the different people in my networking group. All these people are very good at what they do and have earned my trust. Please look through it while I go finish up with the computers and see if anyone has a product or service that might be of interest to you and your wife."

---

We'll never really know how much money Jack left on the table by not using his business card organizer to create more referrals, but here are some examples:

- Mrs. Thompson would have loved help around the house with cooking and cleaning while carrying the baby and possibly after the baby is born. Dog walks for the family's frisky Labrador would also have been of interest. Putting two and two together, this was a terrific opportunity for his networking group's house cleaner, personal chef and pet sitter.

- If Jack knew the Thompsons lived in a 35-year-old home and had been suffering from dry skin and itchy eyes, he might have anticipated the couple's concern about bringing a newborn baby into the house and would have referred Ernie to his networking group's air duct cleaner and water purification system salesperson.

- In addition, had Jack known that the Thompsons had been too preoccupied to update their financial planning, he could have created a flurry of business by referring the group's accountant, insurance agent, investment advisor and attorney for Wills and Trusts, to protect the assets of the growing family.

- If Jack had known that the Thompsons were interested in converting the covered patio right outside their master bedroom into a baby nursery, as well as adding a security and fire alarm system, he could have created business for the group's general contractor and security system salesperson.

- Had Jack realized the universal truth about maintaining marital bliss—paying attention to one's wife—when Jack overheard Thompson on the phone, he would have referred him to his group's gift basket maker ("Baby on the way!" basket), jeweler ("Push Gift" bracelet or necklace) and a florist (bouquet and balloon).

In this case, way too much money was left on the table that could have easily been earned had Jack made his Power Team visible using his business card organizer as a tool.

# *A Real Estate Story*

Karen made two sales the very first day her new flooring store was open. Not bad for a start-up business whose owners moved into town not even six months earlier. Although Karen and her husband Mike knew no one locally when they arrived, they *did* know how to run a flooring business. The newlyweds figured their knowledge and expertise was all they needed to succeed!

Luckily, at a Chamber of Commerce mixer, Karen met Debra, an experienced event planner, who was also active in a local business networking group. Debra liked Karen from the moment they met. She asked Karen about her plans for the new store and soon learned that Karen, rather than implementing a pre-launch marketing and promotional program that every new business needs to create awareness and drive traffic, was instead focusing exclusively on making tenant improvements to the retail space they had leased.

As an event planner, Debra specialized in grand openings and product launches for a wide variety of businesses, and she quickly outlined a simple plan to help Karen hit the ground running when the new store opened its doors. Karen realized the wisdom of Debra's plan and agreed to meet with the group's website designer, graphic artist, and promotional products expert to start her branding process.

Next came meetings with the group's banker, bookkeeper, printer, computer pro, and other business services specialists who could help Karen with the daily operation of running her business.

But the key to the plan was a well-publicized grand opening to bring prospective customers into the store. All thirty-two members of Debra's networking group promoted the event through their personal and professional spheres of influence, and the result was a grand opening that exceeded even Debra's optimistic projections.

The event featured delicious foods from her caterer, floral arrangements from the florist, and complimentary limousine service to shuttle local designers, contractors and home builders back and forth from their offices to the store. Debra's expert use of her network not only made the grand opening a hit, it created a lot of business for many of her networking partners.

In the two months before the grand opening, Debra had asked Karen to attend the weekly early morning meetings of her networking group, to meet her colleagues face-to-face. Even more generous, a slot was open in the group for a flooring specialist—and the group only allows one person per profession.

Debra explained that getting involved in the group would be a great way for someone like Karen, who was new in town, to build a business through word-of-mouth referrals.

Debra outlined how it worked. Karen's customers, people installing new flooring, will in many cases be remodeling or building a home, and as a result, a targeted prospect for many of the businesses in Debra's networking group. By creating business for the network, Karen would certainly receive a good deal of business in return.

Although Karen appreciated the invitation, she was too overwhelmed to even consider attending a business meeting, particularly one so early in the morning. She told Debra that once the store was open and things calmed down, she would make it a point to visit the group as Debra's guest.

As the grand opening wound down, after the last customer had gone and the caterer had cleaned up and left, Mike locked the front door, walked into the back office, and compared notes with his wife. Looking back on the day, Karen and Mike were tired, but thrilled. They received two purchase orders which would cover the expense of the grand opening, as well as next month's rent and then some. Yes, the business was off to a great start and life was good!

At least that's what Mike and Karen thought. As great as the day turned out, it could have been much better. They didn't realize it then, but Mike and Karen both overlooked several opportunities during the grand opening to create big business for Debra's networking partners, which in turn would have ultimately come back to them in the form of reciprocal referrals.

Why were these opportunities overlooked? Simply because Karen or Mike hadn't yet invested the time and energy to join the group, learn how word-of-mouth referrals work, or start building relationships.

One example of a missed opportunity were the Palmers, a husband and wife who came into the store to check out prices of hardwood flooring for a new custom home they were planning to build in the next six months. Too busy to talk at length and have a meaningful conversation, Karen failed to ask a few easy questions that would have revealed that the Palmers were actively looking for a Realtor to help purchase a vacant lot with great views, as well as a general contractor they could trust to build their dream home.

As it turned out, Karen simply wished them good luck with the new house and went on her way mingling with other customers on the showroom floor. Karen, by not thinking things through, left a lot of money on the table.

## Overlooked Referral Opportunity

Chet Palmer is one example of a referral opportunity that could have been uncovered. Chet is a retired attorney with a total budget of $500,000 to purchase a home site and build the new construction home. His plan was to pay $150,000 cash for the land and take out a mortgage to finance the $350,000 balance. As part of the construction package, the general contractor could hire a variety of members in the networking group as vendors and subcontractors.

That would have been a terrific opportunity for his networking group's Realtor, loan officer, insurance agent, general contractor, heating and air conditioning specialist, air and water purification systems professional, interior designer, furniture salesperson, landscaper, and security system salesperson, to name a few.

This example is only one of many overlooked referral opportunities during the flooring store's grand opening. In total, a staggering sum of money was left on the table, money that could have been earned by members of the business network. In the process, Karen and Mike could have earned the credibility that leads to receiving referrals in return.

Karen eventually spoke to Debra about visiting her networking group, but by then someone else had filled the flooring business position. Not only was Karen a day late and a dollar short on creating referrals for the Palmers, she had missed out on an ongoing stream of referrals from a terrific group of local business people. As a result, Karen left more money on the table than she will ever know.

# A Relocation Story

When Marla first started in real estate twenty years ago, she missed more opportunities to create business for her networking partners than she now cares to recall. Back then, Marla didn't know a thing about networking. She graduated with honors from a prominent business college, but there weren't any courses offered on networking or referral marketing.

Everything Marla learned about referrals came from a business networking group she joined soon after beginning her career in real estate. Becoming active in a structured networking group was the best career move she ever made. Things started slow, but that's the nature of the real estate profession. Buying and selling property is a high-dollar, high-risk transaction. Rarely do "ready, willing and able" clients appear out of thin air for a new agent.

Marla's work was cut out for her. As a real estate rookie and new member of the group, referrals did not come overnight. It took several months for the other members to gain trust in Marla. But as she began to build relationships, meeting one-on-one with the other members and growing their business by passing referrals, her colleagues began to respond to Marla's Givers Gain® approach by referring buyers and sellers to her.

Everyone who worked with Marla gave glowing testimonials about her professionalism. Within a year, Marla's real estate career was doing very well. Business generated directly from her networking group earned Marla "Rookie of the Year" honors at her office. In subsequent years, Marla was a consistent top money earner and award winner for her brokerage, relying almost exclusively on word-of-mouth referrals to build her business.

Along the way, Marla found that she enjoyed helping people move into town, not only to purchase the right house at the best price, but also to help her clients adjust to living in a new location. Marla invested time and money in continuing education and received several certifications as a "Relocation Specialist."

The year Marla was named her company's top income earner, she said, in her remarks from the podium at the awards dinner, "I made it a point early in my career to take a proactive stance with every single client or prospect I work with to use a system that actively promotes the people in my network and their business. I have learned the importance of making my network visible.

I train my clients to see me as a directory for local products and services they can trust. People moving into a new location need almost everything you can imagine! Not only do they love me and refer their friends and family to me for the help I give them, but all the people I network with truly appreciate the ongoing business I send. In return, they also create as many referrals for me as they can."

The secret to Marla's success is actually the **World's Best Known Marketing Secret**. She has a word-of-mouth networking system in place and uses it consistently. For example, Marla understands that people relocating to a new location have a diverse range of needs, so she put together a simple brochure with a brief description of all the products and services that her network offers. Marla also makes a point to take a few minutes and go over the brochure with her clients, offering powerful, firsthand testimonials (and a business card) for any business in which her client expresses an interest.

Although no single client has ever used all of her networking partners for one relocation, it's the rare client of Marla's who hasn't worked with at least one. That's right: almost every single client to whom Marla has sold a home in the last twenty years has done business with one or more of her networking partners.

Here's a partial list of the business categories for which Marla created referrals over the years:

| | | |
|---|---|---|
| ▪ Accountant | ▪ Florist | ▪ Loan Officer |
| ▪ Air & Water Purification | ▪ Furniture Sales | ▪ Massage Therapist |
| ▪ Attorney | ▪ Gift Baskets | ▪ Nutritional Products |
| ▪ Auto Repair | ▪ Greeting Card Sales | ▪ Office Machines |
| ▪ Business Coach | ▪ Heating/Air Conditioning | ▪ Personal Chef |
| ▪ Caterer | ▪ Home Inspector | ▪ Personal Trainer |
| ▪ Chiropractor | ▪ Insurance Agent | ▪ Pet Sitter |
| ▪ Cleaning Service | ▪ Interior Design | ▪ Photographer |
| ▪ Computer Repair | ▪ Jeweler | ▪ Printer |
| ▪ Errand/Delivery Service | ▪ Landscaping | ▪ Security Systems |
| ▪ Event Planner | ▪ Life Coach | ▪ Telecommunications |
| ▪ Financial Planner | ▪ Limousine Service | ▪ Travel Agent |

Of course, we'll never really know how much money Marla took off the table and deposited into her networking partners' bank accounts over the years. In fact, the actual dollar amount doesn't matter. Success speaks for itself. And in this case of Marla systematically implementing her word-of-mouth referral strategy, it thunders loudly!

# Chapter 3

# *Power Team Concepts and Terms*

**W**hy are some people better networkers than others? Because they know more people? No, though being well-connected certainly helps. Knowing many people does *not* automatically translate into many referrals.

How about "people" people? The type of person who strikes up a conversation anytime, anywhere, with anyone even if just for a minute. No. Confidence and the ability to talk to strangers increase the **number of opportunities to create a referral**, yet while millions of great conversationalists can talk and talk on interesting subjects, few are able to consistently generate business for someone else.

So if being well connected and the gift of gab are not guarantees of successful networking, what skill separates the people who create an ongoing stream of money-making referrals from those who don't?

Simply put, great networkers see opportunity where others do not. They connect the dots and find money on the table that others miss.

## The First Dot

**The First Dot –** the point that alerts you to the opportunity—is to recognize that *people going through a Key Situation always have a need*. In some cases, they haven't yet realized what those needs are or had the time to find a solution.

**Dot –** New baby? Have you looked into life and health insurance? Or have you had your air-conditioning ducts cleaned for the baby's room? What about a chiropractor and massage therapist who specialize in prenatal body work for new moms?

**Dot –** You're building a business? You're probably already working with a terrific computer pro as well as a top-notch CPA for your taxes and expenses. But have you thought of how a personal chef might save you time and money?

Unfortunately, most people *consistently* miss referral opportunities. They believe they're trying to network by attending mixers and other functions, but nothing ever seems to happen for them in terms of creating business at these events. In fact, many people in structured networking groups *designed* to build each other's business leave way too much money on the table as well.

Why? Because people fail to recognize opportunities.

We have found that the best way to recognize opportunity is to give it a name and a face you can remember, which triggers your brain's Reticular Activating System (RAS). That's the area responsible for regulating arousal and sleep-wake transitions, in other words, waking your brain up so it can remember. That's where the Six Key Situations come in.

Even more basic than recognizing opportunity is finding it. Or better yet, creating it.

How?

By asking questions.

Here's what one networking and referral expert believes:

---

### *Hazel Walker – BNI and Referral Institute: "The Power of Questions"*

*"He who controls the questions controls the conversation, so I'm always asking questions. I want to know about people:*

- *'What are your biggest challenges this year?'*
- *'What obstacles are you trying to overcome?'*
- *'What's keeping you up at night?'*
- *'What did you accomplish this year that you are really proud of?'*
- *'How can I help you?'*
- *'Who do you need to be connected to?'*

*The constant questions help me uncover their needs and ultimately, how I can help solve them!"*

## The Second Dot

**Dot** – Great networkers are not only skilled at uncovering a prospect's needs, they are also **prepared to help by referring business people they like and trust** as the best person the prospect could call for help with that particular need.

But there's more to creating referrals than simply asking questions, recognizing opportunity and having a team of professionals on hand.

**Great networkers take action**, connecting the dots with an effective, enthusiastic and compelling recommendation explaining to the prospect what makes that networking partner special, and why the prospect will benefit from that connection.

Here's an example of successful networking in action:

### James Hamilton – ADT Security Systems : "Pushing Buttons and Referrals"

*"Brian is a carpet cleaner in one of the Manhattan chapters of BNI. He called me one day to tell me about a new office building for an import/export company. He noticed that when people walked in and out the receptionist had to interrupt her activities and enter a code to let anyone in – including employees and visitors.*

*As Brian was getting paid, he struck up a conversation with the owner. 'You ought to think about getting one of those systems where employees tap a card against a reader and the door opens automatically. That way the receptionist won't be continually getting interrupted.' Brian said.*

*The owner replied, 'That might be good in the future, but I don't know anybody who sells that type of system.'*

*'I can get someone for you to talk to right now,' Brian said, 'so then later on when you are ready, you can get it installed.'*

*Sure enough, it was an Access Control System, which we carry. It turned into a great new client for us!"*

# Power Team Terms

Our ultimate goal is to create a *Power Team* of networking partners who generate an ongoing stream of money-making referrals for your business. These networking partners are the most active and productive group of business referral partners you can have.

Let's start building the Power Team conceptually and include concrete examples from people who've employed some of these concepts. Ultimately, we will go through all 36 of the most popular and common business categories that make up referral networking groups.

## Power Term Number 1: *Key Situation*

**Concept:** A **Key Situation** is a specific lifecycle event typically being experienced by a group of consumers who are targeted prospects in a variety of distinctly different target markets.

Every business person knows *what* a target market is, but surprisingly few know *who* makes up his or her target market. Or, better yet, how to find them. Even fewer business people have a grasp of how to recognize targeted prospects for their networking partners.

We will identity six everyday Key Situations which help to recognize referral opportunities by putting an easy-to-recognize face on the targeted prospects for your networking partners, regardless of which industry group they belong.

As a result, you will never miss these opportunities again.

In some cases, finding money on the table is as simple as recognizing less obvious and potentially powerful relationships between businesses *that appear to have nothing in common.*

Some examples:

> **Caterers** (Events) and **Life Insurance Sales** (Finance) can both provide a valuable product or service to targeted prospects in the "Getting Married" Key Situation.

> **Printers** (Business Services) and **Pet Sitters** (Personal Services) both provide a valuable product or service to targeted prospects in the "Business Builder" Key Situation.

> **Massage** (Wellness) and **Home Security** (Property Services) can both provide valuable products and services to targeted prospects in the "New Baby" Key Situation.

In short, the Six Key Situations are common threads that each of your networking partners can weave into an efficient, effective, and ever-expanding tapestry of top-notch referrals for the entire group.

---

### Mike Macedonio – The Referral Institute:
#### "Key Situations and Target Markets"

*"When you look at an event to help identify a target market you broaden the target of what you train your networking partners to look for in the pursuit of creating referrals. I think it's a powerful technique because it shows people how to identify events that lead to referral opportunities, both giving and receiving.*

*When we start using events, it simplifies the process of identifying a target market. This is a great place to start but it is a one-dimensional approach. If we do an assessment on your business as a company and you as an individual, you'll find there's a lot more to it. One of the things we do at the Referral Institute is a deeper analysis of the individuals themselves. What's driving them? What are their values? What were some of the key events when they were growing up that shaped them?*

*We get down to a point with them at their core that gets emotional. At that level, at the core of their values, their competencies, what they do, and how and why they do it, it becomes more clear on who they want to serve and who they want to work with.*

*The other part comes down to their capacity to actually reach and serve a particular target market. For example, if you are a one-man show you may only have the capacity to work within your city or state. And there are many other variables that come into play when we get at this level of detail. The value of getting down to this level really becomes evident when they start making business decisions, such as where am I going to invest my time and money to build the business?*

*At the same time, however, when you select a target market it doesn't preclude you from doing business with people outside your specific target market. That opportunity still exists. It just gives you a central focus on where to put your energies, time and money.*

*Most people don't have time or money to do the type of research and analysis that I'm talking about. For most business people, I think that this methodology of looking at these key lifecycle events opens peoples' eyes to the enormous number of opportunities that exist everywhere* around them. Power Teams work because people are taking the next step and going deeper with the relationships. The fact that people are taking the additional effort to advance those relationships, and in many cases, advance from visibility to credibility, produces more success."

Later in the book, we also focus on additional *custom* Key Situations you can train your networking partners to recognize and convert into even more referrals. But before we get there, we first need to create business for the others, motivating them to go the extra mile for us. Here's how one networking trainer helps her students identify their target market.

---

### Tiffanie Kellog – Referral Institute: "Target Markets"

*"We start by asking, 'What is your target market?' and we almost always get someone who says, 'Anybody, Somebody and Everybody.' As a result, we spend a decent amount of time narrowing it down into specifics, like 'I'm looking for pregnant women,' or 'I'm looking for chiropractors in a particular area of town.' Once we are able to do that, we are going to have a lot more success.*

*When we get too broad with the target market, many of our students struggle with determining the really good referral sources for them. For a business it's very easy to say great referral sources would be a CPA or a financial planner. So we try to come up with new ideas and be creative.*

*Last week, we had a student who is a massage therapist. In determining his target market we found out that good Contact Sphere relationships for him were bicycle stores and a running club. These were totally different target markets than we would have originally considered. So we really work on getting as specific as possible with what the target markets are."*

## Power Term Number 2: *Network*

**Concept:** The term **Network** describes all of the businesses with which, and people with whom, you have connections or maintain a certain level of visibility. *Visibility is when someone knows who you are and what you do, and you know who they are and what they do.*

Everyone you've ever met in person or have a direct connection to online, over the phone, or otherwise, is a potential or established network partner. Network partners can be the source of something you need in one of three areas:

- **Referrals** – Business Opportunities

- **Information** – Expertise and Experience

- **Support** – Help and Encouragement

Your network, which is also known as a **Sphere of Influence**, is made up of people who, at a minimum, will know who you are when you contact them.

## Power Term Number 3: *Contact Sphere*

**Concept:** The term **Contact Sphere** describes a group of business professionals in non-competing, complementary, symbiotic business categories.

Examples:

- Florist, Caterer and Photographer

- Chiropractor, Massage and Nutrition

- Realtor, Mortgage and Insurance

Understanding how your business fits into time-tested relationships among *Contact Spheres*—business categories which traditionally pass referrals back and forth—is critical to the formation of your Power Team.

Knowing your own Contact Sphere, and which business categories your Contact Sphere is missing, makes it easier to find the networking partners you need to build your Power Team.

## Power Term Number 4: *Power Team*

**Concept:** The term **Power Team** describes the people with whom you have a relationship that are symbiotic and complement rather than compete with your business **and** have made a mutual commitment to actively engage in a referral relationship.

The key differentiation distinguishing a Power Team from a Contact Sphere is the higher degree of mutual commitment and increased level of networking activity taking place.

## *Diversify For Success*

*Unlike* a simple Contact Sphere or industry group in which even the least skilled or marginally motivated networker is an occasional referral "Order Taker" for a related business (such as Realtors for the mortgage officer, massage therapist for the chiropractor), a diversified Power Team makes the commitment to work diligently together to find money on the table by creating more business for each other regardless of whether or not they are in related businesses.

Examples:

A jeweler who recommends a CPA and attorney specializing in estate planning to every young couple purchasing a wedding or engagement ring (part of the "Wedding" Power Team).

The air conditioning contractor who always recommends a nutritionist to every customer who's hired the contractor to clean out air conditioning ducts and install air filtration systems as a way to help stop sneezing, coughing and itchy eyes (part of the "Allergy" Power Team).

## *Contact Sphere = Networking Platform*

Business people are looking for more business. Now! Not later. The sense of urgency is palpable. But overnight success stories are rare. In most cases, it takes between five and ten years to become an overnight success.

Advertising is no quick fix. Consumers suffer from information overload, numb to a sales pitch from any person or business to which they are not already connected. More than ever, people will strongly prefer to do business with people they *already* like and trust.

Not too long ago, before the Internet, when someone needed a new product or service he or she asked friends and family for their opinions, or scanned the Yellow Pages, hoping for the best. Now anyone can go to Twitter or Facebook and ask for referrals in real time while performing due diligence online through a variety of search engines and consumer review web sites.

Information is abundant but the source is more important than ever. *You and I will always gravitate toward doing business with people we like and trust.* That's true if you're building your business online, in person or over the phone.

## Power Magnet

The same is also true in reverse. People you have never met will contact you to do business *if someone they know and trust gave a strong enough recommendation* about you. Particularly if the referral source is in a business related to yours. Say a florist recommends a caterer or a business coach recommends a website specialist or marketing guru. Makes sense, right?

So let's start building your business by networking *strategically* with other businesses that work for the same client as you, businesses that will complement what you are doing without becoming your competition. Let's start creating your Power Team referral network.

Ideally, the people on your Power Team will act as your "Bragging Buddy," a networking partner who makes the prospect, in many cases their current client, understand that you are the best possible person he or she could work with for the particular product or service you represent.

The chart below represents six common Contact Spheres with six popular business categories for each:

### Six Contact Spheres

**Events**
Caterer
Event Planner
Limousine Service
Photographer
Jeweler
Florist

**Real Estate & Finance**
CPA
Attorney
Insurance
Investments
Mortgage
Realtor

**Wellness**
Chiropractor
Personal Trainer
Air/Water Purification
Nutrition Products
Life Coach
Massage

**Property Services**
Cleaning
Furniture Sales
Heating/Air Conditioning
Security Systems
Interior Design
Landscaping

**Business Services**
Business Coach
Mobile Telecom
Thank-You/Follow Up
Computers/Internet
Office Machines
Printing

**Personal Services**
Pet Sitter
Errand/Delivery
Auto/Body Repair
Greeting Cards
Personal Chef
Travel Agent

©2011 by Ivan Misner and Money on the Table Book

Illustration 3A

## Start With Your Contact Sphere

Your business fits somewhere into one of these six time-tested Contact Sphere relationships, groups of business professionals in non-competing, complementary and symbiotic businesses that traditionally pass business referrals back and forth. Knowing which Contact Sphere you are in, and which business categories your Contact Sphere is missing, makes it easier to find some of the new networking partners you need on your Power Team.

## Where Do You Fit?

Illustration 3A is an example and limited to only six business categories per Contact Sphere. Many businesses could easily fit into one group or another and many more are not shown.

If you are in a profession not listed, choose the Contact Sphere that seems most applicable. Whatever Contact Sphere you choose will not limit your networking efforts. We simply have to start somewhere, so please just make the selection you feel best fits your situation. Once you finish this book, you'll have the skills and insights to develop your own customized Contact Sphere.

# Chapter 4

# The VCP Process®

Think of the sales process, in particular, selling your product or service. Picture yourself walking up to a stranger, introducing yourself and diving right into your best sales pitch. To make things more interesting, let's say you get lucky and the person is actually in need of your product or service. Maybe they have a bad back and you are a chiropractor. Now, in your mind, try to close the sale without allowing the prospect time for research or due diligence. Simply picture yourself asking the prospect to take a leap of faith and do business with you, or in this case get a spinal adjustment right then and there.

We all know this approach is doomed to failure. Unless you're selling food to the hungry or drink to the thirsty, it's going to take a little more than hanging out a shingle to seal the deal. Let's switch things up a bit. Now instead of you walking up to a stranger and launching into a sales pitch, imagine one of your Power Team partners talking to the same person, and the two are coworkers who have known each other for many years. In conversation, the prospect gives an audio cue that he is a targeted prospect for your business. In this example, he complains of a backache and you are a chiropractor. Recognizing opportunity, your Power Team partner proceeds as your Bragging Buddy with the same sales pitch you used earlier in this example.

Clearly, there is no comparison between the paltry success rate of cold-calling a stranger to create a sale and the high closing ratio that results from a compelling referral given by someone the prospect knows, likes and trusts.

## There is No "I" in VCP

Generally speaking, people don't take kindly to a sales pitch from a stranger. Call it "invisibility." There are far too many choices for consumers in our wired world of information to do business with someone we know nothing about.

Business is all about relationships—the deeper the better. It doesn't matter what type of business you are in. Your networks for information, support and referrals will drive your success, and the strength of those networks is based on your relationships with other individuals and businesses.

Power Team networking develops deeper and stronger relationships by focusing on a mutual benefit for both parties, and involving many different types of relationships. Among the most important are the relationships with your Power Team partners and the prospects these referral sources bring you.

## Ivan's Perspective
### *"Premature Solicitation"*

*"Have you ever been solicited for a referral or for business by someone you didn't even know? Michelle Villalobos, a BNI member in Miami, calls this "Premature Solicitation." [Say that fast three times and you might get in trouble!]*

*I agree completely with Michelle, and I've been a victim of "premature solicitation" many times. I was recently speaking at a business networking event and, before my presentation, someone literally came up to me and said, "Hi, it is a real pleasure to meet you. I understand you know Richard Branson. I offer specialized marketing services and I am sure his Virgin enterprises could benefit from what I provide. Could you please introduce me to him so that I can show him how this would assist his companies?"*

*Okay, so what I was thinking was:*

*Are you completely insane? I'm going to introduce you, someone I don't know and don't have any relationship with, to Sir Richard, whom I've only met a few times so that you can proceed to attempt to sell him a product or service that I don't know anything about and haven't used myself? Yeah, right. That's NEVER going to happen.*

*I am pleased to report, however, that with much effort, I was able to keep that little monologue inside my own head, opting instead for a much more subtle response.*

*I replied… "Hi, I'm Ivan, I'm sorry – I don't think we've met before, what was your name again?" That surprised the man enough to make him realize that his "solicitation" might have been a bit "premature." I explained that I regularly refer people to my contacts, but only after I've established a long-term strong relationship with the*

> *service provider first. He said thanks and moved on to his next victim.*
>
> *Networking is not about hunting. It is about farming. It's about cultivating relationships. Don't engage in "premature solicitation." You'll be a better networker if you remember that.*
>
> *– Dr. Ivan Misner*

## VCP Process®

Relationships do not instantly appear out of nowhere. They must be nurtured from the tender seeds of networking. Relationships evolve through mutual trust, shared benefits and what we refer to as three phases of growth: **Visibility, Credibility**, and **Profitability**. We call this evolution the **"VCP Process®."**

Any successful relationship, personal or business, is unique to the individuals involved. A relationship begins with unfulfilled possibilities and expectations. It grows stronger with experience and familiarity. It matures into trust and commitment.

The VCP Process® describes the creation, growth and strengthening of business, professional and personal relationships. We use it to assess how a relationship fits in the process of referrals. It can be used to foster the growth of a rewarding relationship with a prospective friend, client, co-worker, vendor, colleague, or even family member.

## Visibility

The first phase of growing a relationship is visibility: you and another individual become aware of each other. In business terms, a potential source of referrals or a potential customer becomes aware of the nature of your business, perhaps because of your public relations and advertising efforts, or perhaps through someone you both know.

This person may observe you in the act of conducting business or relating to the people around you. The two of you begin to communicate and establish links – perhaps a question or two about product availability. Initially, you may become personally acquainted and work on a first-name basis, but you know little about each other.

A combination of many such relationships forms a casual-contact network, a sort of *de facto* association based on one or more shared interests. The visibility phase is important because it creates recognition and awareness. The greater your visibility, the more widely known you will be, the more information you will obtain about others, the more opportunities you will be exposed to, and the greater your chances of being accepted by other individuals or groups as someone to whom they can or should refer business. Visibility must be actively maintained and developed; without it, you cannot move on to the next level: credibility.

## Credibility

Credibility is the quality of being reliable and worthy of confidence. Once you and your new acquaintance begin to form expectations of each other – and those expectations are fulfilled – your relationship enters the credibility stage. If each person is confident of gaining satisfaction from the relationship, then it will continue to strengthen.

Credibility grows when appointments are kept, promises are acted upon, facts are verified, and services are rendered. The old saying that actions speak louder than words is true. This is very important. Failure to live up to expectations – to keep both explicit and implicit promises – can kill a budding relationship by creating the type of visibility you don't want.

To determine credibility people often turn to third parties, seeking the opinion of someone who has done business with you. Are you honest? Are your products and services effective? Are you someone who can be counted on in a crunch?

---

### Peter George – Marketing Coach: "Internalize Givers Gain®"

*"Some people come into a networking group like BNI and hear about "Givers Gain®" but they don't internalize it. They see all the referrals being passed and all the Thank-You's going back and forth, which draws them in. But they will be disappointed if they get into the mindset of just showing up and expecting that to happen.*

*I like to show them the "VCP Process®." It astounds me when you get someone who's been in business for 20 years and you give them that concept and they say "Oh, wow what a great idea!" Dr. Misner put the term "V-C-P" out there – but it's not a new philosophy.*

*I try to show people that "Givers Gain®" is truly the way it's done. I tell them, "You are here to make money but you are going to make money by helping other people do the same." There's a reason terms like "What goes around comes around," and "You scratch my back and I'll scratch* yours" and now "Givers Gain®" have been around for a long time. But the concepts only work if you internalize that philosophy and go out and live it."

## Profitability and Time

Mature relationships, whether business or personal, can be defined in terms of "profitability." Is it mutually rewarding? Do both partners gain satisfaction from it? Does it maintain itself by providing benefits to both? If it doesn't profit both partners to keep it going, it probably will not endure.

The time it takes to pass through the phases of a developing relationship is highly variable. In a time of urgent need, you and a client may proceed from visibility to credibility overnight. It's not always easy to determine when profitability has been achieved – a week? a month? a year?

Profitability may happen quickly or it may take years—most likely, somewhere in between. It depends on the frequency and quality of the contacts, and especially on the desire of both parties to move the relationship forward.

However long it takes, when you have established an effective referral-generation system, you will have entered the profitability stage of your relationships with many people—the people who send you referrals and the customers you recruit as a result.

## Sales and Referrals from Inside and Outside

You know you have an opportunity to move toward credibility when your networking partners begin to do business with you, buying your product or using your service themselves. In Power Team terms, this process is known as an "Inside Sale," members doing business with other members. If you do business together again, and continue the relationship, you have a greater chance to reach credibility with your networking peers. Inside sales are great because they give your networking partner a firsthand testimonial as your Bragging Buddy.

## Ivan's Perspective
### "Credibility is a Mutual Feeling"

*The fact that you do business with a Power Team member helps build your credibility with someone but it is not a "referral" in the sense that most people understand a*

> "referral." A referral involves a recommendation to a third party as opposed to one Power Team partner purchasing the products or services of another, which is a sale. Regardless, both inside sales and referrals are an important opportunity for building credibility.
>
> Do not, however, make the assumption that you have credibility with someone just because you are doing business together. One person may see the other as being credible. The second person, however, may not see the first as credible. If that happens, you are not at credibility. Both parties must agree. The fact that one person is doing business with the other does not mean that the relationship is at credibility. The relationship can only operate at whatever level <u>both</u> sides think it is.
>
> – Dr. Ivan Misner

## Lisa Jordan – Accent American Cleaning and Disaster Restoration: "Inside to Outside Referrals"

"We received a referral from the Realtor in our chapter for a water-damage situation at a property she had listed. We completed the remediation work and worked with the insurance company.

The insurance adjuster, Rich, was very impressed with our work as well as our ability to estimate the jobs accurately.

Rich began referring us to his clients. He referred us approximately $100,000 in new business in a year. Rich then introduced us to another adjuster in his company, Chris, who also began referring us to his clients. Rich then introduced us to Matt, another adjuster, and Chris introduced us to Kevin, who is also an adjuster from their company. Matt then introduced us to yet another adjuster from their company named Tammy.

All told, the revenue generated from that one referral from two years ago has made us over $250,000 gross revenue and is still growing. With recent rains in Tampa, we had 23 jobs going on at the same time, 19 of them referred by one of these adjusters.

On remediation jobs, we need other people as well, so the general contractor in our chapter gets a piece of nearly every referral. We have also called in the AC contractor, the electrician, the house painter, and the house cleaning service from our chapter. If we had a plumber, he'd be getting calls also, but the referrals are going to a plumber in another chapter.

In our meetings, when any of us have thank-you dollars, we just refer to the referral that keeps on giving. The general contractor has had to hire three additional people to keep up with the work. The air conditioning contractor, who has been in our chapter four months, has reported a business increase of 30% already."

## Ivan's Perspective
### "Expectations and Business Categories"

*In many ways, a fast rise up the "Time Confidence Curve" is more about the person than the profession. I've seen people in professions that generally take a long time to hit profitability on the confidence curve shorten the timeframe. But the time-confidence curve generally holds true and, as a rule, a florist is going to get referrals faster than an investment advisor investing retirement income.*

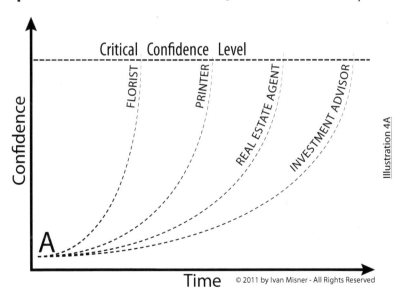

Illustration 4A

*Sometimes people stumble over someone who needs their services right away, even though they've just met, but that's a rarity... even a blind squirrel can stumble over a*

> *nut! But stumbling over business is not what we are talking about with networking, which is really about going deep and building relationships.*
>
> *When you are focused on building relationships, the confidence curve becomes a science, and you can move it one direction or another depending on how good the individual is, but it is mathematically accurate that a florist is going to get referrals quicker than an investment advisor.*
>
> *When you give a referral, you give a little bit of your reputation away. If you give a good referral, you enhance your reputation. A bad referral will hurt your reputation. If I give you a referral to a florist and they don't do a good job, my reputation may be tarnished a bit but it is not completely destroyed. If I refer you to an investment advisor who runs away with all your money, our relationship is over.*
>
> *– Dr. Ivan Misner*

## Everything Counts: Build Trust and Increase Performance

How you are seen by others has everything to do with how many referrals you receive. Like it or not, everything you do and everything you say either helps or hurts your personal brand, even little things you rationalize in your mind as unimportant or unnecessary.

Power Team referrals are based on trust. Your Power Team partners must be confident that you are going to make them look good in the eyes of the customer. If not, you've received your last referral.

People gain trust in each other when they see a pattern of solid performance. Some people evaluate each other based on the best price or whether the person has the most experience. Other variables are personal, such as appearance or personality. Whether we realize it or not, we all judge others based on appearance. We are judged by what we talk about as well. People who spend a lot of time complaining, or dwelling on negative topics, will not receive as much Bragging Buddy promotion from their networking partners as other people in the group who are upbeat and fun to be around and have a sense of modesty and decorum.

*Beth M. Anderson – BethMAnderson.com: "Everything Counts"*

*"You are always doing a commercial, whether you realize it or not. People are always watching you and making decisions based on how you look, how you present yourself, as much as what you actually do. People have different triggers of what they respond to and we all need to be at least aware of what they're putting out there."*

## Power Team Report Card

There are many factors that will determine if, and when, you gain your Power Team partners' trust. Here are a few particularly helpful best practices if you belong to a structured networking group with a regularly scheduled meeting.

1) **Be good at what you do.**

2) **Arrive early to the networking meeting.**

3) **Introduce yourself and mingle with visitors.**

4) **Change your sales force update week to week,** describing the targeted prospects you want the Power Team to find for you this week. Tip: be very specific. Spend more time on what you want, not so much on what you do.

5) **Carry a Business Card Organizer** stocked with a few of each networking partner's cards. Review it every morning and focus for a moment on each member and their services. You will give more referrals.

6) **Give at least one quality referral a week.** Write referrals as they happen and call your Power Team partner as soon as possible. Don't wait for later.

7) **Give at least one quality testimonial a week.** Thank another member in front of the group for doing a great job with a client on a referral you gave, or tell the group about one thing you learned about another member during a face-to-face meeting that will help you find more referrals. This is particularly effective if favorable comments from an "outside" customer are quoted to the group, and very helpful to new members seeking to reach credibility.

8) **Be sure visitors you invite do not conflict with a current member,** when inviting businesses from open categories to join your Power Team. If there is a potential conflict, call the member to discuss and, if necessary, have the member talk to the prospect directly.

9) **Follow up on referrals** that you receive in a timely manner. The speed with which you follow up on a referral has a direct impact on your closing ratio.

10) **Thank referral givers.** People appreciate recognition more than we realize. Thanking referral sources is an important step in staying top-of-mind and building long-term networking relationships. Best case scenario: use the products and services of your networking partners as thank-you gifts.

11) **Dress to meet or exceed expectations for your occupation.** You only have one chance to make a first impression.

12) **Avoid negative comments.** Don't badmouth the competition, even in general, vague terms. Focus on the positive aspects of your product or service.

13) **Engage in open networking.** Open networking events are the life blood of a Power Team. Get out there and meet somebody!

14) **Do a face-to-face meeting at least once a week** with another Power Team member to increase the quantity and quality of referrals and learn more about each other's business.

Use the Power Team Report Card for a more detailed checklist and scoring system to keep track of your networking activity and identify networking skills you can improve to increase the number and quality of referrals you give and receive! (See appendix page 230 or for a full-size, printable version of the Power Team Report Card visit www.moneyonthetablebook.com)

### Power Team Report Card

| Do I..? | REGULARLY | SOMETIMES | RARELY |
|---|---|---|---|
| Arrive early or on time for my networking group meetings — | | | |
| Introduce myself to visitors at the meetings — | | | |
| Prepare my Sales Force Update in advance — | | | |
| Alternate the Targeted Prospects I train my Power Team to recognize — | | | |
| Meet individually with other Power Team members — | | | |
| Successfully train Power Team members to give compelling testimonials — | | | |
| Diligently seek Bragging Buddy opportunities for my Power Team — | | | |
| Carry a stocked and current business card organizer — | | | |
| Give high quality referrals to meet or exceed group standards — | | | |
| Invite potential networking partners to meet with the Power Team leader — | | | |
| Follow up quickly on referrals I receive — | | | |
| Keep referral sources updated on follow up activity — | | | |
| Exceed client expectations and consistently make referral sources look good — | | | |
| Thank people who give me referrals — | | | |
| Keep the Power Team up to date with my current marketing tools — | | | |
| Dress to meet or exceed expectations — | | | |
| Maintain an enthusiastic and positive attitude — | | | |
| Engage in Open Networking Opportunities — | | | |
| Invest time in personal development & communication skills — | | | |
| Invest time in professional development & communication skills — | | | |
| Total | | | |
| | x5 | x3 | x1 |
| Scores | | | |
| TOTAL SCORE | | | |

**Scoring System**
95+ Power Team Hall of Famer
85+ Power Team All Star
70+ Power Team Role Player
60+ Power Team Bench Warmer

Illustration 4B

### Kristie Smith – Realtor: "Thanking Referral Sources"

*"Things don't get done unless there's a system for it. For example, when we get a lead, any type of lead, everyone on our team knows that the first thing we do is ask, "How did you hear about us?" So that is part of everyone's first initial conversation we have with them.*

*If the prospect came to us by way of a referral, regardless of if I know the person who gave us the referral or not, we immediately run what we call a "Lead Series" in our contact management system and it triggers us to send the referral source a handwritten note thanking them for the referral. We'll send a Starbucks card, or other types of gift cards. We have a little box of them always ready to go and we try to rotate what we send.*

*If someone refers to me a lot, we look into our database to see what we sent them last time, if I sent him a Starbucks card last time I'll do something different this time. Regardless of whether or not a referral turns into business, we always, always thank and gush with appreciation for the referral.*

*If it does turn into business, we always thank the referral source again. We might give something a little bigger like a dinner night out, or if it's a close referral source I know personally, then I can get more creative. We have a section in our database for hobbies, favorite restaurants, other specific things they like. For example, they might be big Notre Dame fans here in Indiana, so I might get them a Notre Dame welcome mat for their new home, or something a little personalized, if I know them well enough and know what they like or are interested in."*

# Chapter 5

# Order Takers, Connectors and Creators

D r. Hugh Needatwist is a chiropractor who built his business with word-of-mouth referrals, as did Manny Goodbuys, the Realtor in his Power Team business network. These two networkers are from different industries – health and wellness and real estate and finance – but players in these two different fields can generate a lot of business for each other.

## Order Takers

As Manny the Realtor is showing homes to a middle-aged couple from out-of-state, the conversation ranges from children and pets to local restaurants. When the topic turns to local doctors, the husband asks Manny for a good chiropractor. "My back is killing me," he says. "I'm going to miss Dr. Popalot back in Toledo."

Turns out the couple was in a car accident several months ago and have been under regular chiropractic care for neck and back injuries. As is often the case, *clients moving into a new town ask their Realtor for recommendations* on everything from restaurants and pet sitters to eye doctors and, yes, chiropractors.

Manny instantly becomes Dr. Needatwist's Bragging Buddy and tells his clients about his chiropractor networking partner. "Dr. Hugh Needatwist is great! He's the only chiropractor I let work on me and on my family. Here's Dr. Needatwist's card. Would you like me to have him give you a call?"

In this scenario, Manny is an order taker. In other words, after someone asked him a direct question – "Do you know a good chiropractor?" – all Manny had to do to create a referral for the chiropractor is *respond to the question.*

## Connectors

The next day, at the real estate office sales meeting, Manny notices that one of the other agents is in obvious discomfort, walking with a limp and rubbing his neck. Manny asks what happened and his fellow agent tells him how he slipped off a ladder while painting, and has been in pain ever since.

"You need a good chiropractor," Manny tells him. "My chiropractor, Dr. Hugh Needatwist, helps lots of injured people relieve pain. In fact, I see him myself. He's very gentle and can help relieve your pain so you feel better without prescription drugs. Would you like Dr. Needatwist's card or can I have him call you?"

In this case, Manny is a "Connector." He saw someone in obvious pain, made the connection that the chiropractor can help, and instead of leaving money on the table, *Manny took action, asking the prospect if he would be interested in the chiropractor's services.*

## Creators

Later in the day, Manny is at a Chamber of Commerce mixer. One of Manny's friends introduces him to a personal injury lawyer.

As a result of meeting regularly to learn about each other's business, Manny knows that the chiropractor would like to be introduced to personal injury lawyers, since lawyers are a potential "Golden Goose" who can send an ongoing stream of business to the chiropractor, not to mention the massage therapist and other members of the networking group.

After small talk, Manny becomes the chiropractor's Bragging Buddy, a referral "Creator." He doesn't just see money on the table, he creates it!

Manny says in an *enthusiastic* tone, "I do a lot of networking with someone you may be interested in meeting. In fact, he's the only chiropractor I let work on me and my family. Doc Needatwist is just a really nice guy and he's very good at what he does."

Manny is now poised as a referral sharpshooter. Target in sight, he carefully takes aim before pulling the trigger questions. "Dr. Needatwist told me he is looking for a personal injury lawyer to refer business, since some of his patients ask for personal injury lawyer recommendations. Would it be okay if I gave Dr. Needatwist your card so you two can discuss *referring business back and forth*?"

## Bragging Buddy and Three Levels of Referrals

Got your notebook? Let's nail down four very important terms:

**Bragging Buddy** – A networking partner who helps a prospect like, trust and *want to do business* with you.

**Order Taker** – Passive Bragging Buddy who reacts to a direct question: "Do you know a good chiropractor (or lawyer, therapist, etc.?)"

**Connector** – Active Bragging Buddy who recognizes a visual cue (someone limping or in obvious discomfort) or a target phrase ("I fell off a ladder," "Car Accident," "Pain") and approaches the prospect as his networking partner's Bragging Buddy.

**Creator** – Proactive Bragging Buddy who recognizes and approaches a Golden Goose source of ongoing referrals for the Power Team.

## Business Categories in Your Industry Should All Be Order-Takers

Mastery of the basics takes practice. Networking is no exception. Turning people in related businesses into order takers for your business is a critical first step in building your Power Team.

The reason? People in related but non-competing businesses are already working with your targeted prospects. The process is simple. Be a Bragging Buddy to your clients for the Power Team partners in your industry, create a lot of referrals, and your Power Team partners will do the same for you.

After all, satisfied clients come pre-sold! You were hired to do a good job. Exceed expectations and you are viewed with admiration, someone the client likes, trusts and wants to help. Can you say, "V-C-P?"

Unlike connectors and creators, being an order taker requires less creativity and more of an ongoing system. *But like the others, order takers need training to be effective.*

*In addition to getting your networking partners to like and trust you, they need to <u>take action</u> to help you by making the Power Team visible and talking to their clients about you.*

### Jim Munro – *Munro Graphics: "Copy Machines to Nonprofits"*

*"Bob Westcott of CopiLabs is a great guy and he really works hard to help out his buddies. He introduced me to the Deputy Director of a nonprofit here. He was actually trying to sell them a new machine, and while they weren't interested in it at the time he always made it a point to get into a conversation about what they were doing, what their problems were and how he might be able to help them.*

*The Deputy Director of the nonprofit mentioned that they were working on their annual report, which involves a lot of printing, and he said, "I know this great printer here in town. I'd like to give him your phone number to see if he can do something for you."*

*I gave them a call and didn't hear back from her right away. About five weeks down the road, I did get a call from her. They were ready to move forward on their annual report. Afterward, they were very satisfied with our work.*

*That was about three years ago. In the meantime, the Director of this agency is also the Treasurer of the Lawrence Historical Society, and she made sure that I got their work. She's also involved with a couple of private schools and she suggested they pass on their work to me. There have been at least six or seven different nonprofits that she has brought into my customer base – and it all started with the initial referral from Bob to her. It really is the gift that keeps on giving and that one referral probably represented 50 percent of our growth last year.*

*Bob tends to put a personal face on things. He tries to set up a referral by saying things like "This is a great guy, somebody that you really ought to talk to!" In my case, it wasn't anything specific about my business that Bob told the Director, he just spoke about me being somebody he knows, likes and trusts. I guess the fact that I bought two copiers from him made me likeable!*

*After that first referral and getting to know what the nonprofit is all about, I became an advocate for them because I really believe in what they do. But the most important reason she keeps referring me (and I know because she's told me), was our responsiveness to their needs.*

*For example, they were working on a project last summer when I happened to be on vacation. My associate here worked with them. It was a very small job and my associate had already gone home for the day. She happened to catch me on the deck at my beach house and asked "Is there any way you can make this happen for us?"*

*So I got hold of my associate, who went back to work and took care of them, which really sealed the deal for us with them. It was a very small project, but it was a very important project for them that had to be taken care of that day."*

## Beyond Your Industry Sits a Golden Goose

Networking with another business that serves the same targeted prospects extends beyond the business categories in your industry. In fact, this common variable is the X Factor in the entire Power Team equation.

Let's use a different analogy. Every recipe has a critical ingredient that absolutely **must** be included for the concoction to be a success. Forget the vodka and instead of a Screwdriver, you've just got orange juice. Leave out the yeast and your bread comes out like a cracker.

It's the same with networking. There are a few basic ingredients that cannot be omitted in cooking up money-making referrals for your Power Team and, in return, for yourself.

Top of the list: *Golden Goose referral sources from a variety of industries.*

A Golden Goose is usually someone who deals with your targeted prospects on a regular basis and is already in position to create an ongoing source of referrals for you. Keep in mind that a Golden Goose can be from *any business category or from any industry* as long as they are working with the type of clients you are looking for.

---

### James Hamilton – ADT Security Systems: "Proactive Habits"

*"Daniel Jacoby in BNI Chapter 37 in Manhattan is with SDL Brokerage and has given me so much work, I can't tell you how grateful I am to him. He is a property and casualty insurance broker and I get about one referral a week from him that turns into closed business.*

*He makes it a habit to be proactive and tell people, "We have a partnership with one of the ADT Dealerships here in town. If you want to save money on your insurance and protect your home at the same time with a great security system, I can have my good friend James give you a call!"*

## Put On Your Chef's Hat

Let's do a little role playing. Put on your chef's hat and think about the catering business.

As a caterer (in the Events Contact Sphere), you do a lot of business at wedding receptions (the Key Situation is: "Getting Married"). You may also do business with other categories in the industry – a jeweler, florist and event planner and so on. Through networking, you can recommend each other to your clients to make more business for everybody. So far, so good.

But plenty of businesses from other industries also come into regular contact with people getting married—**businesses that have nothing to do with the wedding as an event in itself, but everything to do with the couple getting married**.

Among these are CPAs, Realtors, financial planners, hair stylists, massage therapists, interior designers and life coaches. All of these business categories, and others, can send you, the caterer, an ongoing stream of referrals for people getting married. In other words, all are a potential Golden Goose for your business.

Want to do something great for the caterer on your Power Team? Give compelling recommendations to every business person you know who works with people getting married. Tell them about the best caterer in town so they can begin referring business back and forth!

## Feed the Hungry

Keep your chef hat on for another moment and take note. Everyone on your Power Team is hungry for more business. And the more mouths you feed, the more motivated people you have searching for *your* money on the table. *Keep the focus on giving.* Regardless of what's cooking in your business, you will never become a referral gourmet as a one-dish, or one-referral, wonder.

*You must be able to recognize a Golden Goose for all Six Key Situations, not just the Golden Goose for your best Key Situation or targeted prospect.*

We outline specific Golden Goose prospects in Chapters 13 through 18, the *Start Bragging!* section for each Key Situation, as well as in more general terms throughout the next several chapters.

## Chapter 6

# Train the Power Team

Think about your **Target Market**. What do the people in your target market look like? Where do they live? Why are they good prospects for your business? What business categories are already working with your target market? In other words, who are the potential Golden Goose referral sources capable of sending an ongoing stream of prospects to you?

What should your networking partners brag about as your Bragging Buddies?

What target phrases and visual cues should your Power Team be on alert to recognize?

In the chiropractor and Realtor scenario from the previous chapter, the Realtor is from a different industry group (real estate/finance vs. health and wellness) yet is able to *connect* and *create* referrals because the chiropractor has successfully trained the Realtor to recognize money on the table when he sees a targeted prospect, someone in obvious physical discomfort, as well as in a Golden Goose business category, such as a personal injury lawyer, and then also follow through by offering the prospect a chance to connect with the chiropractor.

As a Power Team partner, it is your responsibility to train your networking partners to recognize Key Situation opportunities to create referrals for you.

---

*Peter George – Marketing Coach: "Commitment to Training"*

*"A Power Team takes the next step forward after Contact Spheres in making obvious referrals come to fruition. **The big thing with a Power Team is making the commitment to another person** that you are actually going to go out there and sell that service, or promote that product, or help that person and business get where it needs to go.*

*In my particular Power Team, a few of us are deeply committed to helping each other. We get together at least once a week and contact each other if not every day, at least every other day. Over time, we've learned as much about each other's business as possible."*

## Connector to Creator Worksheet

The Connector to Creator "C2C" worksheet organizes the Six Key Situations into a simple format, streamlining the process of training your Power Team to recognize and convert previously untapped opportunities into business for you.

**Connector to Creator Worksheet**

These are the Six Key Situations. Select the three you feel are most appropriate to your business.

☐ BUSINESS BUILDER  ☐ RELOCATION
☐ GETTING HEALTHY  ☐ NEW BABY
☐ GETTING MARRIED  ☐ REAL ESTATE

Last Name / First Name _____
Telephone Number: _____
Business Category: _____
Scope of Products & Services: _____
_____
_____

| KEY SITUATION | Key Situation 1: | Key Situation 2: | Key Situation 3: | Custom Key Situation 1: | Custom Key Situation 2: | Custom Key Situation 3: |
|---|---|---|---|---|---|---|
| GOLDEN GOOSE: | | | | | | |
| BRAG ABOUT: | | | | | | |
| | My _____ is someone I like and trust as a person because: | | | Everyone I talk to who has worked with my _____ says: | | |
| LISTEN and LOOK FOR: | | | | | | |

Illustration 6A

The idea is that you and your Power Team partners exchange <u>already completed</u> C2C worksheets at face-to-face meetings as a quick and easy way to cross-train and learn about each other's products, services, differentiated value, success stories and targeted prospects. As a result, you will become more effective Bragging Buddies for each other's business.

Of course, face-to-face meetings are an ongoing process. Reviewing each other's C2C worksheet is imperative during the first few meetings. Later, your face-to-face meetings will evolve into building deeper relationships, which we cover in Chapter 10, *Power Team Action Grid*. (See appendix page 228 or download the full-size, printable version of the Connector to Creator worksheet and other forms at www.moneyonthetablebook.com)

Let's focus on each section of the C2C as it relates to your business.

## The Golden Goose

Once you have identified the Key Situations that work best for your business, you can then recognize the people and businesses that are potential Golden Goose referral sources for you.

Using the Golden Goose categories discussed throughout this book, as well as any others you come up with on your own, identify and help your networking partner take note of Golden Goose referral sources for each of your best Key Situations.

## Brag About!

In the "Brag About" section of your C2C worksheet, list the benefits to the customer that you bring to the table for any given Key Situation. Remember to stay with short bullet points on *what you want your networking partners to say as your Bragging Buddy when talking to prospects.*

**Be sure to match the benefit to the Key Situation.** For example, if you are in the real estate business and you are targeting first-time buyers and couples in the Getting Married Key Situation, you will train your Power Team to tell this group of prospects that you are "great at explaining the process to first-time buyers and making sure all details are handled correctly," as well as that you "love working with newlyweds who are combining households and have a house to sell."

If you are prospecting for the Relocation Key Situation, you may want to train your Power Team to brag about you as the "local area expert and a great negotiator, someone you can trust to know the town like the back of his hand and get you the best price and terms on the right house, in the right neighborhood."

DO NOT RUSH through this exercise! Boiling down the benefits of your products or services for each of your best Key Situations into short, easy-to-remember bullet points is critical to helping you train the members of your Power Team to be an effective Bragging Buddy.

What do you enjoy most, or get the greatest satisfaction from, when working with people in this Key Situation?

 **Power Team Training Tip:** *Help your Power Team remember a short success story to tell as your Bragging Buddy.*

### James Hamilton – ADT Security Systems:
### "Hair Salons, Paintings and Neighbors"

"Judy Gittenstein is a content provider and member of BNI Chapter 7 in Manhattan. The owner of her salon lived in the same building where the salon itself was located. While the salon owner was doing her hair, he mentioned to Judy that his insurance company required that he get an alarm system for a painting he owned that was valued at over $100,000.

Judy said that she had the very person for him—me. When I called him, he said, "Yes, Judy told me about you and she told me about a few different people she knows who are happy with your security systems. When can you come over?" Of course, that sale was closed before I even got there!

About a month later, he referred me to a neighbor of his in the same apartment building. My client told one of his neighbors that with a burglar alarm and fire detection system you get a discount on homeowner's insurance. I called him, made the appointment and closed that sale.

The interesting thing to me was that it was a content provider leading me to a hair salon, then to a neighbor who otherwise was someone I never would have done business with."

## Listen and Look For

Target phrases are common, everyday statements, expressions and other audio cues the Power Team is trained to recognize as money on the table and an opportunity to create a referral. Visual cues can also be powerful, yet simple triggers to help your Power Team recognize opportunities to create referrals for you.

Come up with a few target phrases and visual cues to help your networking partners see your money on the table. What should they listen and look for?

### Patrick Finley – Art Promotional Services, LLC: "Be Specific"

"I try to be very specific when I ask my networking group for referrals. One time I asked for an introduction to a guy, Craig Lyle, who is in the marketing business. A woman in my networking group happened to be on LinkedIn one day and saw that a gentleman that she was connected to was connected to Craig.

*She called this gentleman and said, "Would you mind giving an introduction for a referral partner of mine named Patrick to Craig Lyle?" He said, "No problem, just have Patrick call me." That resulted in a good deal of business for us!"*

## Custom Keys

Whether your business is a perfect fit to uncover targeted prospects and money on the table for your business with one or more of the Six Key Situations, or a stretch to find even one that pertains to your business, all businesses have additional, more narrowly focused types of targeted prospects that create many incoming, money-making referrals.

**Think of the Six Key Situations primarily from the perspective of giving referrals to a wide assortment of business categories.** The greater your understanding of the benefits and value your networking partners bring to the Six Key Situations, the more effective you will be as a Bragging Buddy and the greater the number and quality of referrals you will create.

Even if *your* business can't generate referrals from any of the Six Key Situations (which we think is impossible), seize the opportunity to create VCP Process® currency in your favor with the Power Team by bringing as much business to as many networking partners as you can.

Now let's dig into additional, more narrowly focused or "Custom" Key Situations you can train your Power Team to recognize and convert into money-making referrals for you.

---

*Tiffanie Kellog* – *TiffaniKellog.com: "Custom Targets"*

*"Many times people say that as a promotional products person my Contact Sphere should have a design company, graphic designer and website designer, but I'm targeting chiropractors and I'm looking for radiologists and physical therapists, massage therapists and nutritionists to lead me to the chiropractors. I've focused my networking on a very specific target market and I look for the people who are doing business with them."*

## Follow the Format

Train your Power Team to recognize your Custom Key Situations with the same C2C format as the Six Key Situations. Breaking your message down into a Key Situation, Golden Goose, benefits, target phrases and visual cues, greatly increases the Power Team's retention of your custom key message.

As you come up with custom keys for your business, print out the Custom Key Worksheet from www.moneyonthetablebook.com and complete the "Golden Goose," "Brag About" and "Listen and Look For" sections of the form.

Here's an example of how one businesswoman managed to employ a "Brag About" benefit and "Listen and Look For" target phrase. Mary, a Realtor, likes working with "empty nesters," those couples whose children have grown up and moved out of the house.

The Golden Goose referrals Mary sees as the most direct way to reach empty nesters are the wellness industry business categories, including all forms of healing modalities who help the aging homeowners with health issues, and also financial planning business categories, who can assist with estate planning and other money-related issues.

The benefit that Mary wants her Bragging Buddies to brag about is specific to the interests of empty nesters: "Mary sells for top dollar and loves working with seniors!" Finally, the target phrases Mary wants the Power Team to look and listen for are "Our house is too big," "The kids have all moved out," or "We want to downsize."

## Face-to-Face

In addition to sales force updates at a structured networking meeting, or 60 second commercials, sales manager moments, or elevator speeches as they are sometimes called, Power Team members always benefit greatly from good old-fashioned human interaction in the form of one-to-one, face-to-face meetings.

## First Meeting

The first meeting between two Power Team partners should be structured. Using a standardized system of communicating with each other is *absolutely critical* for the group's success as the Power Team grows.

Selecting an appropriate location for a first meeting is also very important. The location should be relatively quiet and free from interruptions and distractions so you can hear each other easily.

Ideally, the best place for a first meeting is at the workplace of one of the members, though only if you can meet without interruptions. If a workplace location isn't possible, pick a convenient restaurant, coffee shop or other quiet public setting for your meeting.

Members should schedule *90 minutes to two hours for their first meeting* and should bring the following worksheets, which are explained in this chapter:

- Two *Ten Key Questions Worksheets* (blank)

- Two copies of your *Connector to Creator Worksheet* (already filled out)

- Two *Power Team Action Grids* (blank)

## Meeting Agenda

After you and your Power Team partner arrive at the appointed location and make yourselves comfortable, dig into the details of your first face-to-face meeting.

Use the following agenda to keep the meeting on track:

- Interview each other using the *Ten Key Questions Worksheet*. Take 15 to 20 minutes each, for a total of 30 to 40 minutes.

- Exchange and discuss *Connector to Creator* and *Custom Key Message Worksheets*. Take 15 to 20 minutes each for a total of 30 to 40 minutes.

- Review the *Power Team Action Grid*. Take a total of 20 to 40 minutes.

## Ten Key Question Worksheet

Use the following ten-question sequence to interview your Power Team partner. The goal is to *learn what makes your networking partner special as a person,* as well as how to recognize your Power Team partner's best prospects. As a result, you can be an effective Bragging Buddy. As a Bragging Buddy, your job is to help prospects *like, trust and want to do business* with your Power Team.

Here are the Ten Key Questions, as well as tips to using each question effectively:

1) **How did you get started in your business?** This is a great icebreaker question. Sometimes knowing what motivated your networking partner to get into their particular business enables you to give stronger testimonials about him or her.

2) **What do you enjoy most about what you do?** Telling a prospect that your networking partner loves what they do and why, with details and stories, is very important in helping the prospect "like" your Power Team partner.

3) **What separates you and/or your company from the competition?** You are looking for "bullet points" that can be told quickly and easily to the prospect to illustrate *why you can be trusted* to do a good job.

4) **What advice would you give someone starting out in your business?** Asking someone for advice shows respect and is essential for building credibility with your networking partner on the road to profitability.

5) **What are the coming trends in your business or industry?** If your Power Team partner has detailed information and strategies on how to profit from upcoming trends, you might learn something of value. Conversely, if your networking partner is too preoccupied with daily business to have any input here, it is an opportunity for you to help them with any trends you see that might affect their business. Build rapport by taking an active interest in your Power Team partner's business.

6) **What strategies have you found to be the most effective in promoting your business?** This question leads to brainstorming for each other's business and stimulates the exchange of marketing and promotion ideas, as well as business building in general.

7) **If there was anything about your business or industry you could change, what would that be?** This question, in addition to building rapport, allows your Power Team partner to discuss business freely and provides you with the opportunity to suggest solutions or at least gain a better understanding of the challenges they face.

8) **What is the next big event coming up for you?** This question almost always results in referral opportunities if followed up correctly.

9) **What is your biggest challenge at the moment?** The answer will provide insight into your networking partner's business and life to help you understand him or her more as a person, as well as possibly uncovering money on the table with referral opportunities for the Power Team.

10) **What type of customers are you looking for? How will I recognize a good prospect for you? Which Key Situations are your targeted prospects experiencing?** Okay, fine, this is really three questions! In essence, the more vivid picture your networking partner paints of who and what they are looking for, the greater the probability of you recognizing their targeted prospects, giving a compelling testimonial and creating a money-making referral.

A copy of the Ten Key Question Worksheet is included in the appendix page 227 or visit moneyonthetablebook.com to download a printable version.

## More Key Question Tips

- Follow up on the other person's answers with another question or two to really delve into their thoughts and more importantly, their feelings.

- Use questions that begin with: Who, What, When, Where and Why, to uncover a wealth of information that will help you give more powerful testimonials to generate referral opportunities.

- Take notes on the Ten Key Question worksheet as your networking partner is answering the questions.

- Keep a notebook with a section for each Power Team member for future reference.

## Exchange Worksheets

After completing the Ten Key Questions take out the *Connector to Creator Worksheet*. Review your partner's Connector to Creator worksheet and talk about each of the Key Situations and targeted prospects.

Specifically, learn the following:

- Which Key Situations do they want me to look for?

- What Golden Goose referral sources do I already know (or can I find) who do business with the targeted prospects they are looking for?

- What Key Situation benefit can I get excited bragging about to prospects?

- What makes my networking partner "special?" Is there a short testimonial or success story to tell prospects?

- What phrases should I listen for, or visual cues should I look for, to find their targeted prospects?

## Custom Keys

Repeat the same sequence with each other's Custom Keys Worksheets. In addition, ask yourself and your Power Team partner:

- Do you have a connection to each other's custom keys?

- Do any of the other current Power Team members have a connection to any of these custom keys?

- Who do you know in open business categories that have a connection to these custom keys?

---

*Lisa Jordan* – *American Accent Cleaning and Disaster Restoration :*
*"Face-to-Face Meetings"*

*"You never know where a referral is going to come from. We had a member of our networking group, Tom, who sells a new type of air decontamination equipment, mainly to large industries and disaster restoration companies like ours.*

*He had a one-on-one meeting with the jeweler in our networking group, and the jeweler referred him to another restoration company. The company was working on a large fire loss, and was looking at having to destroy millions of dollars in inventory due to smoke odor. Tom convinced the company to try his machine on the job site, with the understanding that if it didn't work, there would be no charge.*

*Within three days the smoke odor was completely eliminated, all of the inventory was saved. Tom made over $145,000 from that one referral and was invited to the annual meeting of the restoration company—a major franchise—and given a booth to show his equipment. Tom was promoted to VP of his company immediately after that."*

## Face-to-Face Again and Again

It has been said that networking is a "contact" sport. It's also an ongoing activity. Situations change, but if you know what you are looking for, opportunity is everywhere:

- Be sure to update the Power Team on new Key Situations or Golden Goose referrals that will benefit your business.

- Meet regularly with your Power Team to update and keep the group informed and focused on what you are looking for.

- Do as many face-to-face meetings as it takes to become an order taker for the people in your Contact Sphere and they will become order takers for your business as well.

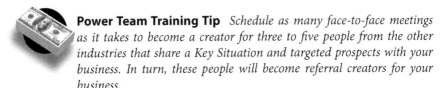 **Power Team Training Tip**  *Schedule as many face-to-face meetings as it takes to become a creator for three to five people from the other industries that share a Key Situation and targeted prospects with your business. In turn, these people will become referral creators for your business.*

You must first gain the trust of your Power Team partners. But trust alone is not enough. Always remember that people will be more motivated to build your business if they like you. And nothing builds friendship more than a little quality time face-to-face and making money for each other!

## Things to Talk About

For success in generating referrals, it's crucial to know your sources—the members of your network. As such, there are five topics of critical information that members of your network should know about each other.

These five topics are not mysterious secrets. We are exposed to them every day, but often pay little attention to them because we are not aware of the benefits we can accrue by sharing them. *Business by Referral*[2] calls this type of sharing the GAINS Exchange:

- Goals
- Accomplishments
- Interests
- Networks
- Skills

---

2    *By Robert Davis and Dr. Ivan Misner (Bard, 1998)*

If you know the GAINS categories and use them effectively, you can strengthen your relationships, create strong organizations and live a more rewarding, productive and enjoyable life. The exchange is a two-way street. Not only should you know these things about others, you should share the same type of information about yourself with them.

## Goals

Goals are the financial, business, educational and personal objectives you want or need to meet for yourself and for the people who are important to you. These could be problems you want to resolve or decisions you need to make, either immediately or down the road.

Whatever these objectives are, you need to define your own goals clearly and specifically. You also need to have a clear picture of the other person's goals. Indeed, the best way to develop a relationship is by helping someone achieve something that's important to him or her. If you do, they will remember you when you need help achieving your goals. You will become valuable resources for each other and your relationship will endure.

## Accomplishments

Sometimes the deepest insight into others comes from knowing what goals they have achieved, what projects they've completed, what they have accomplished both for themselves and for others. Actual accomplishments— whether as a student, employee, organization member, parent, friend, athlete, sports fan, artist or neighbor—tell you more about a person than any number of intentions or attitudes.

People like to talk about the things they're proud of. Engage your network members in casual conversation; encourage them to talk about their accomplishments. Sharing your accomplishments may lead to fortuitous surprises, such as a mutual interest, or connection that can be beneficial for both of you.

## Interests

Your interests—the things you enjoy doing, talking about, listening to or collecting—can help you connect with others. People are more willing to spend time with those who share their interests.

Knowing other people's interests makes it easier to help them in some way. Let them know your interests, as well. If you and your contact share many of the same interests, it will strengthen your relationship. In either event, these interests make you more human, more accessible, more of a "person" than a "business." Don't forget that your passions are your most important interests. A passion is something you love to do, something you could do all day long without encouragement or prodding from others.

## Networks

A network starts with any group (formal or informal), organization, institution, company, or individual you associate with for either business or personal reasons. Most business people have a broad network of contacts. The question is: How well cultivated are those contacts?

Each of us has sources in abundance that we don't effectively cultivate. Each member of your network is part of several other networks; each of your prospective sources is connected, directly and indirectly, with hundreds, even thousands of people you don't yet know. If you can tap the resources represented by your network of contacts, you can significantly increase your return on investment in networking.

## Skills

The more you know about the talents, abilities and assets of the people in your network, the better equipped you are to find competent, affordable services when you or someone you know needs help. Think about what you do well and identify the special skills you have; exchanging this information with others will help business relationships grow as well.

## Recording the GAINS You Discover

You can gather information about the GAINS of your prospective network members or anyone else you may deal with in several ways. You should:

- Listen
- Observe
- Ask questions
- Review written material
- Share your GAINS

To help you in this process, use the GAINS form in the appendix (or www. moneyonthetablebook.com) to complete GAINS profiles for yourself and your networking partners.

## Take the GAINS Test

If you think that getting to know the GAINS of the people you deal with is too easy and you need a greater challenge, take the quiz at www. moneyonthetablebook.com or see page 232 in the appendix to test your knowledge of each member in your network.

As you discover the GAINS of the people you are interested in, keep a record; otherwise, you're likely to forget important information. Use the GAINS Profile (or whatever database you utilize) to record the facts you learn about your most important contacts. Spend more time with the people you already know, particularly with those you would like to know better.

Concentrate on learning the five GAINS essentials. Find overlapping areas of knowledge and interest and make sure you give back the same kind of information. The more they know about you, the faster your name will come to mind when an opportunity arises in which your products, services, knowledge, skills or experience might play a part.

---

### Beth M. Anderson – BethMAnderson.com: "GAINS Profile"

*"I really like the GAINS Profile. It's a great structure. When people meet for the first or second time there is a tendency not to know where to go with the conversation. There's a chance that when you connect with the person you can spend three hours with them and regret afterward that although you really had a good time, you walked out without the information you need in order to help build that relationship. So if you follow the program, and you make sure that each person gets half the time to talk, you walk away with a real solid foundation to start finding referrals for each other."*

**Chapter 7**

# Big Triggers –
# Prospecting Questions

Power Team networkers know that building a business with word-of-mouth referrals is more about "farming" than "hunting"—more about nurturing relationships and cultivating credibility over time than the one-and-done, churn-and-burn cycle of today's hype-driven mass marketing.

That said, here are three words of war that typically strike fear into the heart of a dove (and bloodlust in the belly of the hawk) that we are going to redirect into the peace and love, good karma, Givers Gain® philosophy we hold so dear. Ready? Aim…

## Targets, Triggers and Bullets

- **Targets**  As in *Targeted Prospects*. Which Key Situations do you want your Power Team to find for you?

- **Triggers**  Questions that your Power Team asks the target in order to **uncover a need** leading to a money-making referral. For example: "What's the biggest challenge right now with your upcoming wedding?"

- **Bullets**  Key bullet points your Power Team shares with a target in an **enthusiastic and compelling recommendation** that explain what makes you special, and **why the prospect will benefit** from working with you.

Okay, now that we've got some terms to play with, let's put the concepts into perspective.

## Targets = Six Key Situations

Your ability to recognize targets that stare you in the face every day, yet you continue to overlook, starts by setting your networking radar to alert you when you come across, or hear about, anyone in the *Six Key Situations*:

- Business Builder
- Getting Healthy
- Getting Married
- Having a Baby
- Relocation
- Real Estate – Buy/Sell/Build/Remodel/Maintain/Manage

## Triggers = Questions

Now you know what to look and listen for. What's next? Pull the trigger! *Ask a trigger question that will uncover a need* and create a money-making referral for someone on your Power Team.

## Bullets = Value

Once a need is uncovered, your ability to hit the bullseye with a powerful recommendation that consistently turns into business for your Power Team depends on *how well you know your Power Team and how strongly you believe their business gives value* to the targeted prospect in any of the Six Key Situations.

## Find Target, Pull Trigger

The search for money on the table begins when you set your networking radar on alert for the Six Key Situations. That's your first task, but waiting around for people to mention that they or someone they know is getting married (or going through any one of the Six Key Situations) and *then* pulling a trigger question is a slow draw. Too slow. Yes, you will occasionally give some good referrals, but the idea is to give *a lot of great referrals on an ongoing basis.*

Recognizing a referral opportunity is not about luck. It's about skill. And it requires focus, as well as intention. Are you motivated to create high volume, high quality referrals for your Power Team? Yes? Here's a secret: Opportunity is around the corner waiting to meet you!

## Two Big Triggers

So rather than sitting back, waiting for people experiencing the Six Key Situations to cross your path, be proactive and start searching. How? Talk to people and get in the habit of asking the following two "big" trigger questions in every conversation:

- "What is the next big event coming up for you?"
- "What is your biggest challenge at the moment?"

Whatever the other person says in reply will lead you to a referral opportunity. How well you play the role of Bragging Buddy for your Power Team will dictate the amount of money on the table your Power Team partner will deposit into his bank account.

Commit the **"Biggest Challenge"** and **"Next Big Event"** trigger questions to memory, use them regularly and they will transform your life as a Power Team networker.

---

### John Chichester – Financial Planning:
*"Is that a Relationship You Want To Continue?"*

*"I'm always listening for an opportunity to refer somebody. I give a lot of referrals at meetings with clients or on the phone. I'm like, "Hey, what's going on?" and they tell me what their issues are. I always say, "Do you have somebody that you are currently working with?" If they say yes, I ask "Is that a relationship you want to continue?" or "Is it a good relationship?" Just because they are working with somebody doesn't mean it's a good relationship.*

*From there I say I have somebody that I've used personally or whatever the situation is, and would it be okay if I have that person call you directly. A lot of times, I will also make it a three-way phone call, we may be sitting in my office and I'll say, "Let's see if we can catch so-and-so," and we make the connection there. Other times, I will set up a lunch and that always works out great."*

## Little Babies and Big Referrals

Dave the nutrition guy is talking to Ima Newmom, a young woman in her early 20's, already expecting her second baby within two years of her first. She was referred to Dave by her mother, the Realtor in Dave's networking group. The topic is Ima's lack of energy and finding the best prenatal vitamins.

A top-notch networker, Dave's referral radar is on alert. Why? He recognizes the New Baby Key Situation as one of the biggest Power Team targets he's been trained to look for.

After answering all of Ima's questions, making product recommendations and placing the order, Dave puts away his product information and price sheets. He pauses for a brief moment, then looks into Ima's cheerful but weary eyes. With a simultaneous tilt of the head and slight squint of the eyes, subtly signaling sincerity, he asks, "*So, what is your biggest challenge with getting ready for the new baby?* Are you changing things to "baby-proof" the house, and doing all the planning stuff like writing your Will or a Trust and getting life insurance to protect the baby?"

Suddenly, Ima is a bit less cheerful and a little more weary. Dave hit a nerve. He is poised to help Ima with some of these other, related issues she needs to take care of. And to do *that*, he is about to turn money on the table into money-making referrals for his Power Team!

## Networking Sharpshooter

Dave has not only identified the New Baby Key Situation, he just pulled the trigger with a couple of carefully crafted questions to *expose a need he can turn into a referral* for someone on his Power Team.

It worked. Ima and her husband want to convert a covered patio off their master bedroom into a sitting room to use as a nursery for the new baby. Bingo—a referral for the general contractor!

And yes, Ima and her husband have thought about a Will or a Trust and know they need life insurance, but the young couple have been too busy with everything else to make those arrangements. No worries. Dave's attorney and insurance agent will make the process easy. Same with a few of Dave's other networking partners including the cleaning service, water purification and air filtration vendors who all work together to create a clean, healthy home for the new baby.

Dave has given such compelling recommendations—not only about the products and services, but how much he *likes and trusts the people*—that Ima agreed it was time to get her growing family's affairs in order and meet with Dave's Power Team. In fact, Ima was so eager to get started, she gave Dave permission to have his Power Team members call!

## Lucky Guess?

Why didn't Ima's mom see the connections between her daughter's needs and the products and services of her Power Team? After all, Ima's mom is in the same networking group as Dave the nutrition guy. The reason is that Ima's mom is more of an order taker than a referral creator. She simply overlooked the money on the table. She never asked and Ima never mentioned that among everything else going on in their busy lives, she and her husband were thinking about a room addition, writing a Will or a Trust, or taking out life insurance.

Does that mean that Dave the nutrition guy was simply lucky? Absolutely not. He was alert to opportunities. Dave knew that along with his nutrition business, which is in the health and wellness industry, businesses in the Property Services and Financial Services Contact Spheres also share the New Baby Key Situation as a gold mine of referral opportunities. By asking a couple of trigger questions to expose a need pertaining to the products and services of his Power Team partners, Dave demonstrated masterful use of his networking ammo belt:

- **Find Target**  New Baby Key Situation

- **Pull Trigger**  Ask questions to expose a need

- **Fire Bullets**  Give compelling recommendations that result in great referrals

Wouldn't you like to have Dave the nutrition guy on *your* Power Team? Better yet, wouldn't you like to have a Power Team full of networking sharpshooters just like Dave, regardless of what business they are in?

## Art of a Powerful Testimonial

Power Team networkers give compelling referrals, consistently turning opportunity into business. Real business. We're not talking about passing a slip of paper with a prospect's name and the good old "gave them your card, I hope they call you" cop-out. No, we're talking about creating referrals that leave the prospect convinced your Power Team partner is the *only person they should call* for the product or service they need. In fact, the prospect is so excited, they *give you their phone number* so your Power Team partner can call them and get started as soon as possible.

How do these red-hot referrals happen? Here's the deal: You must give *enthusiastic and compelling recommendations*, explaining to the prospect what makes your Power Team partner *special as a person* as well as *how the prospect will benefit* by working with them. And the best way to quickly get your points across is with a short little story called a *Testimonial*.

---

### Beth M. Anderson – *BethMAnderson.com* :
#### *"Testimonials and Great Service"*

*"Testimonials to me are all about the service part of whatever a person is doing. Take, for example, the people who sell printer cartridges. You can pretty much get that product anywhere. But if the product is also backed up by excellent service, it makes all the difference in the world, such as when someone keeps track of how often you buy, or what you buy, or when you may need it, it's the service that really makes the difference.*

*So when someone stands up and gives a testimonial for another business, you are really lending your credibility to the service that business gives."*

---

## Make It Personal

Testimonials are most effective when they convey your own *personal story* of working with your Power Team partner.

At the same time, it's impossible to do business with everyone on your Power Team. You are not going to sell your house just to have a great story for the Realtor. Likewise, you may have a product or service which some people on your Power Team simply do not need.

That's when you use *third-party testimonials*, stories of other people who love what you or your Power Team partner did for them.

 **Testimonial Tip: You can always talk firsthand about what makes your networking partner special as a person.**

## Do You Believe?

It's one thing to know on a factual level that your Power Team partner is good at what he or she does. But there's another level, an *emotional* level of how strongly you feel they **provide value.** Do you really *feel* it? Do you get excited knowing that the person you refer to them is going to love working with your Power Team partner?

Or, are you relying on a few facts about how long your Power Team partner has been in business and a vague understanding of what they actually do, hoping to convince prospects to take the plunge, follow your lukewarm recommendation and do business? We hope not.

---

**James Hamilton** – ADT Security Systems:
*"Product of the Product – The Professor, Condo Board and 10,000+ Units"*

*"A property/casualty insurance broker referred me to a professor at Hunter College in Manhattan who lives in an area of upper Manhattan called Morningside Heights. We put a burglar alarm and smoke detection system in his apartment. He is also a member of the board of his condominium association and was very pleasantly surprised that the security system only cost $35.99.*

*Several months later he called me and asked, "Can you do a presentation for us on your services?" I was able to get the entire complex, which has over 10,000 residents!*

*And that's not all. The monitoring of the system is priced low enough that they can charge whatever they want to the residents as part of their maintenance fee. It's not unusual for associations to tack on a dollar or two for their own budget to help pay for general maintenance or whatever.*

*About two weeks later, they called and said they needed to update their security in the main offices of the buildings with surveillance cameras for the corridors leading in and out of the public access ways, plus a controlled access system for the employees in management sensitive areas, and also intercoms for all of the residents in all of the buildings.*

*Altogether it was a sale of more than $60,000, plus the monthly income from the monitoring service. It all started from a referral and a personal testimonial from a satisfied customer!"*

## Do Your Homework

As a Bragging Buddy, your primary job is to help the prospect like, trust and want to do business with your Power Team partner. Your success will be a function of how much you yourself like, trust and want to do business with your partner.

In addition to doing business together and having a firsthand testimonial whenever possible, it is absolutely imperative to meet face-to-face with your networking partners regularly. Why? Situations change from day to day, and so do products and services. ***But the best reason is to really get to know your Power Team and to connect with who they know.*** Remember, this is networking; right?

Bottom line: The more up-to-date you are with your Power Team, the more money on the table you will find, and the more money-making referrals you will give—simple as that.

---

### Hazel Walker – BNI and Referral Institute: "Power of a Rolodex"

*"One of the biggest challenges I have with business people is they underestimate the power of other peoples' Rolodex. It's close-minded. I hear this especially from the Business-to-Business people who walk into a networking group, look around and think, "I'm B2B ("business to business") and high dollar and there's nobody here who can help me!" And they walk out. What they have just done is discount everyone's Rolodex.*

*They don't know who I'm sitting with at PTA, or playing golf with. They don't know who my brother-in-law, my mother-in-law or my friends are. I see that happen more than anything when people discount who other people know. It's the same when they only get to know one side of the relationship. They get to know the husband and everything about him, but have they asked where the wife works and who's in her network?*

*There's a tendency to just look at the person, a Mary Kay lady for example, and say "Yeah, she sells Mary Kay, she can't help me." I had a banker in one of my BNI chapters, a good member who's been in the group for a long time. I sent a Mary Kay person to his chapter. He called me up and was not happy. He said, "I don't know why you would send a Mary Kay person, we are doing business-to-business, Mary Kay is just not going to help us, blah, blah, blah…" So I asked that he just give her a shot, you never know who she knows, and that he let her be in the chapter.*

*They let her in. Shortly afterwards, the banker sent me flowers thanking me for the Mary Kay lady who in her first three months there referred over $400,000 in business to him. This was after he had discounted her* *based on the company she works for. I think that is the biggest mistake that business people make: not getting to know people well enough to find out who they know."*

# Chapter 8

# VCP Online?

In **Chapter 4,** *The VCP Process*®, we looked into the three stages of a networking relationship: Visibility, Credibility and Profitability.

- **Visibility** – People know who you are and what you do

- **Credibility** – People know you are reliable and good at what you do

- **Profitability** – People send you business because they like you, trust you and know you will make them look good in the eyes of people they refer to you

Meeting someone face-to-face, watching their body language, the look in their eyes, how they dress and present themselves, is the best way to build deep, VCP relationships with your networking partners.

## VCP Online?

Old-school networkers are sometimes labeled "hunters," notching their well-worn money belt for each business card collected and cold call made. In many cases, this stereotype is warranted. The truth is, many well-intentioned and hardworking entrepreneurs view business simply as a big numbers game: the more people they pitch, the more chances of hitting a home run.

That's why the Internet is so attractive. Networking online has a huge upside for massive, international exposure at little or no cost. Blend in the potential for "viral growth" of your message, people telling other people, and you've got word-of-mouth networking on steroids. At least on the surface.

When computers first came out, people would ask us if the computer would make them more organized. We'd tell people that if they were disorganized now, they would stay disorganized, but at light speed! The same thing is true with networking online. You will not become a better networker just because you are online. But if you understand the process, you will.

From YouTube and Facebook, to LinkedIn and Twitter, the Internet has leveled the marketing playing field. Visibility to a huge audience is more possible than ever before. But here's the rub: while the Internet is very effective for visibility, how can you reach credibility and ultimately profitability, with people you've never met, and in some cases, have never even spoken to?

## Ivan's Perspective:
### *"Online Networks"*

*In my book, **The World's Best Known Marketing Secret**, which was written in the mid-90's, I talked about the six types of networks in which you should consider participating: Casual-contact networks, strong-contact networks, professional associations, service clubs, social organizations, and women's business organizations. Today, I would definitely add a network to this list that has grown substantially in the last few year– namely, "online networks." Online networking is a growing phenomenon. This book includes my updated findings on best practices for online referral-generating protocol.*

*– Dr. Ivan Misner*

# Top 5 Best Practices for Online Networking

There are several ways to develop your word-of-mouth marketing online, but it is important to understand that the foundation of making online networking work for you is still the same—developing relationships with trusted business associates.

How, then, does one go about integrating the technology available to him or her and still be developing networking skills, relationships and trust in an online environment, thereby growing a business through word-of-mouth marketing? There are several ways.

1) **Join one or more online networking communities.** We recommend Ecademy (www.ecademy.com). After joining, participate in the "community" in whatever way you can to best grow a presence at the site. Posting on relevant bulletin boards is a great way to gain visibility, which can lead to credibility and eventually business.

If you are in a live networking group and then join an online networking group like Ecademy, consider creating a regional or national club or sub-community for the members of your group. This will just expand the amount of networking you can do within your own organization!

Keep in mind that it's not enough to just join and have your name on the membership list. You must focus on building relationships with the other members of the community. This is a new concept to some; others realize quickly that you can develop a relationship with people you are meeting in cyber space.

Be active in the community. Post topics on threads that deal with your area of expertise. Respond to others' postings on other threads, if the subject is at all relevant to your area of expertise. The more you are seen, interacted with and talked about, the more visibility on the site you will gain. One note of caution: Don't join too many of these, or you won't be able to be involved effectively enough to build relationships.

2)  **Start a blog or write a regular column for a website or eNewsletter.** Online networking works best when you get plenty of "hits". …if you can start your blog (basically an online diary) on one of the larger blogger sites or online communities, you will create more buzz for yourself. As people read your content and become familiar with you, they will feel like they know you better and that is integral to the networking process. Becoming an expert in an area and writing regularly about it can go a long way towards building your online networking opportunities.

3)  **Develop an eZine for your own company.** Create an email database of your clients, customers and friends and send them regular content that drives them to your website. Be sure that your eZine contains content that has a broad spectrum of interests about your business. You might want to consider working with a professional eZine developer (yes, we can give you a referral for this!). Encourage clients and customers to contribute to your content. In doing this, you will build stronger relationships with them, too, which will, in turn, help to increase the amount of referrals you'll receive.

4)  **Remember that online networking is still about developing trust.** The bottom line when talking about online networking is still the same as with live networking. To drive business to your company by word-of-mouth, you have to focus on developing relationships with people. In our referral organization, BNI, it's about building a relationship with people in a face-to-face environment that builds

trust. That is where a BNI member is coming from when he or she works with another BNI member in their group. From that trust, you feel comfortable referring people. Effectively, that is the same with online networks. However, it may take a bit longer to develop that trust over the Internet.

Although there really are no shortcuts, technology has made it somewhat more convenient to connect with many more people. That being said, we cannot stress enough that those connections are not terribly valuable if there isn't trust, respect and friendship being established.

5) **Online networking has its own cultural norms.** It is much easier to get "flamed" online than in face-to-face networking. When someone asks a total stranger to do business with them in a face-to-face setting it is difficult for the stranger, because of various cultural norms, to respond in an aggressive manner. Mind you, they are still not likely to feel good about the request, but they don't act visibly upset.

None of those cultural pretenses exist online and people tend to overreact (at least it feels like an overreaction), because they are much less likely to respond as bluntly in a face-to-face meeting. We believe that with online networking it feels easier to be more direct. The problem is that the response is also more direct.

So, what's the answer? Fundamentally, the same as with any other network you are developing. Build a relationship before you ask for business. The foundation of trust (as described in #4 above) MUST be there for online networking to be truly successful. Online networking gives you breadth in your networking efforts. It allows you to broaden your reach to anywhere in the world. Just don't forget that trust and relationship building are still as important as ever.

---

*Beth M. Anderson – BethMAnderson.com: "Be Careful Online"*

*"Visibility is just about being out there, being out in front of people, and that's true in face-to-face and online. We all know someone who is at every networking thing that goes on in your town. Whether it's the local parade, a festival or a Chamber mixer, when you see the same person over and over again, and you like what they are saying and you like what they are doing, you move on to credibility that way.*

*You can do that online by being positive and upbeat. The reverse is true, too. You can be visible but not credible if you are always online complaining or whining about something or just being negative or overly critical. That's not going to get you to the credibility phase. So you might have visibility, but it could be in a bad way. You want to be careful with that online because people can't see your facial expressions, there's no tonality in your voice. Language that you use can be read in different ways depending on the reader's perspective. You want to be even more careful online than you might in person. But you can definitely do it.*

*There's also the problem of being visible but not being "there." There's one woman in particular who posts probably half a dozen quotes to Facebook every day. But if you comment on them she never comments back, so there's no interaction. She's just feeding information out and without the interaction you tend to feel there's no real person there.*

*There's also the business of joining various groups. People will get perceptions of you based on the groups you join. Not that it is automatically good or bad. It could go either way. But I think you do want to be aware that other people are seeing what you do, sometimes people from other parts of your life who you didn't realize would be poking around online."*

## Got Something To Say?

Blogging doesn't just happen. There's work involved. In many cases, when there's a job to do, the first tendency is to try to do the job yourself. Sometimes that's good, sometimes not so good.

Consider the wide range of activities needed for an idea that's been spinning around conceptually in your imagination to find its way out of your head onto your blog where it takes on a life of its own.

Adequacy isn't good enough online. Material must be sharp and provide value. The Internet has a huge audience, and reaching that audience is a monumental challenge. These days, most people (except maybe your mom, heirs to your Will, and the family dog) are too busy to care about all the details of your life, your problems and most of all, your opinions.

Don't agree? Look around. People everywhere are dazed and confused from information overload and economic meltdown. Quick reality check: Did you receive more or fewer Christmas cards than last year? The safe bet is fewer. Why? Too much info day-in and day-out has numbed the collective consciousness, tapping the energy needed to communicate to the point of societal distraction and inactivity.

*"For me, LinkedIn is totally business, but Facebook is more 50/50 business and personal. The reason is because in addition to a lot of business people, I'm connected to a lot of friends on Facebook. Like any place, the more people who know, like and trust you, the more they will do business with you. So showing a human face to who you are I think is important on Facebook. People who just talk about business and never post pictures of their kids or talk about where they are going on vacation, I think from my viewpoint are more just there to "get" and not share who they are as a person.*

*For me personally, my passion is sailing, something I enjoy in my off-time, so if I'm out on my boat at sunset I'll take a sunset picture and post it. It gives people a sense of who I am and what I'm doing.*

*Even when I'm posting something on Facebook specifically about business, I try to put a personal spin on it. For example, I might say something like, "I just updated the Maiden Rock Apple's site with the Halloween party information." It's saying they are my client and that I was hired to do work for them and it's promoting them at the same time. It's a very soft-sell approach."*

## Jack of All Twitter – Say What?

In today's world, it's a crapshoot whether or not a friend will read and respond to an email about your personal news, or even return a phone call. Don't take it personally. People are overloaded.

Imagine the degree of magnetic attraction needed to interest cyberspace peeps you've never met, or at least a statistically significant percentage of them, into caring enough about your opinion on your topic of choice to make the effort of visiting your blog.

Anyone launching networking activities into cyberspace should measure their self sufficiency through all of the steps required to create and manage intellectual property promoted online with WordPress, Blogspot, Twitter and others.

Part of the process includes identifying where you need to bring in an expert with real Internet skills to take your online material to the next level. (It's all about networking; right?)

Here are some important criteria to consider:

- Am I creating unique content with my own voice and message?

- Do I have a business angle? Am I creating content online for personal satisfaction or to make money (either directly or indirectly)?

- If I am in business, what is my product or service?

- Am I utilizing all aspects of online media (audio, video, graphics, etc.) to project my message?

- Am I contributing on a regular, frequent basis?

- Am I my own webmaster, creating my own website or blog with DreamWeaver, WordPress or something similar?

- Do I update my blog/website myself?

- Does my blog/website have all the slick bells and whistles, RSS feeds, links, widgets, opt-in offers, PayPal store, etc.?

- Am I promoting my material online with LinkedIn, Twitter, email signature links, Google tags, Facebook announcements, and other outlets?

- Am I promoting my material with word-of-mouth networking by meeting people face-to-face?

## *Be Present*

A well-rounded online presence usually includes at least two, and often several more, of the most popular social networking websites. For starters, a profile on LinkedIn or Ecademy is an essential cyber foundation to start building a business network online.

Viewed as professionalism and core competence, if you don't have a profile online (okay, let's include the more social and less professional Facebook as well), you are facing a credibility challenge with your online targeted prospects. Call it the age of "information entitlement." People expect to see your face, know a little about your background and experience, as well as how to contact you, so they can check you out further if they choose.

Next, you must have a website or blog to showcase you and your work. Coupled with a profile, a web page rounds out the information on your company, products and services, as well as offering a glimpse into your personality and business philosophy.

---

*Beth M. Anderson – BethMAnderson.com: "LinkedIn for Business"*

*"Being a website designer, I think everyone needs a website. It should be professionally done; even if you do it yourself, you do need another set of eyes to look at it, not only for spelling errors and things like that, but to make sure that it represents you as a company.*

*I think everyone in business needs to be on LinkedIn. I just think that's a requirement. It lends credibility to your business, Same with a picture. Statistics clearly show that there's an astronomical difference in how much attention you will get if you have a nice, professional headshot versus just the gray outline of the mystery person.*

*Just as you wouldn't go out without business cards, you shouldn't start a business without being on LinkedIn, which is one of the first places people are going to look for you. I think you can assume that whether you are going out on a date, or your kids are playing with somebody else's kids, or you are going to get a new client, people are going to look for you on the Internet and being on LinkedIn lends credibility to who you are as person.*

*If you want to go to a more advanced level with it, you have to ask yourself whether you have the time to build and maintain a website. If the answer is "yes," LinkedIn can be a great resource and a great place to build yourself as an expert. Get into the "Answers" section, start helping other people get somewhere. If you help other people get what they want, you'll get what you want. If you just go out there and try to sell to people, your experience is not going to be as successful and people are not going to take you as seriously. It's just like the third-party testimonial will get you more business because it doesn't feel like selling."*

## Are You Smelling What I'm Stepping In?

Profile and web page in place, you are now ready for marketing and promotion. Like a restaurant and its customers, your Internet presence only serves a purpose if your targeted prospects visit to sample the goods. And we all know getting people to do anything is a challenge.

Enter Twitter. A visibility machine, Twitter is a mass-text-messaging service where your message will be found by people searching for a key word used in your Tweet, and more importantly, to all the people who opt-in to receive your updates. Let me reiterate: "Followers" choose to follow your footsteps, and in the bargain, smell what you step in. At least online.

And because they've chosen to receive your updates, followers are more receptive to directives, particularly if they are easy and non-threatening, such as clicking a link to your latest blog post, or to view an amazing photo, for example.

In other words, Twitter is a broadcasting mechanism for your personal or professional brand, enabling you to communicate efficiently and effectively with the network you've built. Got something to say? Step up toward visibility and start Tweeting!

---

### Patrick Finley – *Art Promotional Services, LLC: "Business on Twitter"*

*"We've been able to attract some definite business from Twitter. The big thing is just to be human, don't be a robot and post links all the time. You need to interact.*

*I was just sitting there Tweeting one day and a girl from an ad agency sent me a Direct Message saying she saw that I do promotional products and that her company was looking for a new promotional products person. They asked me to come in and interview to see if it might be a good fit for me to be their new promotional products guy.*

*I met with her, did some quotes and some business for her over the next few months and it just went on from there. It was one of those things that came out of the blue, by being active on Twitter at the right time."*

## Follow Me on Twitter!

Yes, the "announcement" function for Twitter is huge. Getting the word out is critical. But Twitter's bigger benefit is the potential for explosive audience growth.

Here's the deal: In addition to the ongoing power struggle of who has the biggest number of followers, Twitter culture includes an informal competition of who can be the first to tell the group about an awesome new (insert any product, service, opinion or news item) which, in turn leads to more people reading your messages. And those new followers tell their people, and so on. It's viral growth.

The result: A growing number of followers can snowball into serious, exponential momentum. For example, it's not unusual for very active Twitter peeps to have a following of tens of thousands of people. Can you say, marketer's playground?

Maybe half of the people who will follow you are folks you decided to follow first, based on recommendations from others. In turn, some of those people responded by following you. Other followers just pop up and join the parade and, unless you ask, you will have no idea what path lead them to your door.

---

### Hazel Walker – BNI and Referral Institute: "Tie Online Networks Together"

*"For me, personal branding online is about establishing myself as an expert, and there's no better place to do that. I can post my writings, I can comment on other peoples' writing, I can post my press release – I can create a lot of visibility. The actual writing and value of what I'm doing leads to building credibility. I've got numerous clients and jobs because of all my Internet postings.*

*It takes time and effort. Unfortunately, too many people get in there and do it haphazardly. They do a little bit of this and a little bit of that and don't really focus on what they are trying to accomplish.*

*For instance, my blog is also my website. I spend a great amount of time writing on that, both from a personal and professional point of view. When people read my blog, they want to know "who is Hazel?"*

*I try to tie my online networks together. My blog is connected to my Facebook, connected to my LinkedIn, connected to Twitter account, so I have a consistent message going out."*

## Join the Conversation

Standing on your Twitter or Facebook soapbox is an easy way to "join the conversation." To be a player on the world's game board, to star in your own movie, the act of participating, engaging, and ultimately communicating with other people moves you and your personal brand from visibility to credibility.

Some of the most common types of updates include:

- What you are doing
- What you think
- News
- Cool links

Don't take this personally, but people only care about what you are doing if they admire you, want something from you, are responsible for you, or love you. Otherwise, you need to be doing something extremely interesting for people to care.

 **Online Networking Tip:** *If you feel compelled to post updates on your daily activities, try to promote one of your networking partners at the same time. Sure, **once in a while** it's okay to go ahead and show a little flair with a comment on the news, pop culture or an overtime victory celebration for your favorite sports team, but generally speaking, focus on promoting your networking partners and keep the personal byplay down to a minimum until you've got a following that cares.*

---

*Beth M. Anderson – BethMAnderson.com: "What's for Breakfast?"*

*"I do have a tendency online to tell people that I'm going for breakfast at my friend Judith's restaurant. But that has more to do with driving traffic to her business. I like to promote other peoples' businesses when it's something I'm doing personally for myself. So whether it's breakfast at the Third Street Deli, or a massage at Body Kneads in Red Wing, those are personal things – but I do them with a purpose."*

## What Were You Thinking?

Please tell us what you think. Of course, what you are thinking about and how well you articulate the vision will dictate if we care. Generally speaking, if you have a thought you think is interesting, you should share it. Chances are good some folks will agree that you've got something valuable to say.

For the less creative among us, Tweeting links to useful or fun websites, as well as news articles, inspirational quotes, jokes or photos you find interesting, are great ways to provide value to the people following you.

Even better, be a Twitter Journalist, reporting firsthand on events and news you are involved in or find yourself in the middle of; now, that's interesting! People living vicariously through your experiences, which they would otherwise never be exposed to, is the stuff that explodes viral growth of your personal brand.

---

*Peter George –Marketing Coach: "Social Networking"*

*"If you get involved with social networking with the intention of simply selling goods, that's no different than if you walk into a business with a stack of business cards and hand them out. No one does business with*

*you that way. You might get lucky every once in a while, but you are not going to make a living that way.*

*The same thing is true with social networking. You can't just go on and say, "Here's what I'm selling." You get involved and you make connections. You aren't going to connect with everybody, but with some people you do. It's no different than making a connection with anybody else at a networking event. You get to know them and if you can't help them directly you may be able to help them by sending them to someone else as a referral.*

*Building business is all done through relationships. Relationships start with hello, and social networking is a great way to say hello to people you may otherwise never meet."*

## Visibility in Action

Interacting on Twitter starts with a reply (@reply) to something someone Tweets. Sharing a similar experience, congratulating an achievement, agreeing or disagreeing on an opinion, or whatever, as long as you are interacting, you are working toward visibility when you reply to another Tweeter.

Subtle point: Everyone following you on Twitter sees when you reply to someone else. So even if you are replying to someone your followers never heard of, your peeps see you working, and you gain big "V" in the process!

Let's crank it up a notch. Did you find someone's Tweet informative or valuable? Share it with your followers by "Re-Tweeting" (RT) the message.

A good RT has two benefits. Not only will you enjoy increased visibility with your followers who appreciate the value you bring to the conversation with an interesting RT, but you jump start visibility and instantly move toward credibility with the person whose message you RT. After all, you are helping the original Tweeter leverage their efforts, and as a part of their promotional network you become valuable to them.

---

*Peter George – Marketing Coach: "Twitter International"*

*"Someone on Twitter asked me about my workbook and I replied. A woman in England saw the reply, contacted me about the book and ordered it. This is a $147 workbook, so it's not an inexpensive purchase. Here's someone in another country who saw me conversing with someone else who she was connected to, and this is someone I didn't even know existed. She saw this conversation going on, she took part in it, and that*

*became a sale. In fact, she has gone on to subsequently make additional sales for me by telling people she knows about the book."*

## Twitter Success Formula: RT x @ (Twitter) = VCP?

A good sign that you are gaining visibility on Twitter is other people replying to your updates. Other Tweeters are obviously taking note of what you are saying and have something to add. Nice!

You know you are navigating the tightrope toward credibility when other people re-Tweet **your** updates. In other words, they like what you have to say and pass along your message and contact info to all the people following them. And if some of *those* people do the same, now you've got the viral word-of-mouth campaign that lures millions of business people online every day.

Two words: Givers Gain®. The more "@replies" and RT's you Tweet, the more people you are interacting with and the greater the chance of those people caring about what you have to say and re-Tweeting it. And the more RTs you get, the greater your visibility and credibility—at least on Twitter.

## Networking with Social Media

From a business perspective, the ideal use for social media is to build your brand and your credibility with the people you are connected with; it's about providing value for your connections and followers. It is important to offer useful information balanced with a little personal insight and whether you're talking about face-to-face networking or online networking, credibility and relationship building is still critical to the process.

**With social media, the key to success is outlining a strategy** that considers the amount of time you can realistically dedicate each day to your online marketing efforts and to be consistent. People have a tendency to get online at random times and start clicking away. Then something mysterious happens to the space-time continuum and all of a sudden two hours go by and they have nothing to show for it! Here's how to avoid falling victim to that trap....have a plan and work it! Write up a plan for how often you will work your social media and for how long.

Sit down and map out a weekly schedule that outlines specific days and times during which you will develop your social media strategy. Figure out what's realistic and what makes sense for your company and go from there. For example, you might schedule yourself simply to post one update at 9 a.m., one at 1 p.m., and one at 5 p.m. daily, and then dedicate ten minutes to responding to comments and direct messages at 10 a.m. and 3 p.m. on Mondays and Wednesdays. On Tuesdays and Thursdays, you might then dedicate ten minutes at 10 a.m. and ten minutes at 3 p.m. to re-Tweeting people's comments that you find valuable and also thanking people for mentioning you or re-Tweeting your posts. This is just an example, but you should definitely take the time to devise a social media strategy such as this that specifically makes sense for you.

Leverage your time! Be sure to utilize the various tools currently available that are designed specifically to save you time in your social media efforts. For example, sites like http://ping.fm, www.seesmic.com, and www.tweetdeck. com are designed to send your social media updates to multiple social networking sites, including Twitter and Facebook, with one click.

Some sites even allow you to link multiple Facebook and Twitter accounts (if you have more than one) to one desktop application where you can post updates to all sites as well as view and respond to your friends' posts on those sites and keep a log of all your past posts. This means no more logging into multiple social networking sites…you can manage all your social networking accounts from one place!

Also, there are sites such as www.cotweet.com where you can schedule updates in advance so your updates will be posting even while you're not online. People who travel often or are locked up in meetings all day find this to be very useful.

Once you have your strategy in place, you will no doubt be eager to start seeing a return on your online networking investment and it's very important to remember one thing: Networking, whether online or face-to-face, is more about farming than it is about hunting. It's about cultivating relationships with people. Bottom line: It takes time. It is about building the credibility of your brand and that doesn't happen overnight.

## *Social Media ROI*

Return on Investment (ROI) is directly correlated to either: 1) dollars spent (online paid marketing), or 2) time and/or effort spent – in saturating and building strong profiles on whatever social media channels are deemed effective for the brand (including blogging). Don't forget that some businesses will benefit much more from spending more effort on "niche" networks that may have less traffic, but more targeted to the brand's ultimate consumer.

If your network is a mile wide and an inch deep it will not be successful. It is important that you create a network that is both wide and deep. You do this by being visible and engaging in the conversation. Over time, this gives you credibility, which leads to building your brand and your sales and will ultimately give you the biggest ROI for your online marketing efforts.

**Most of what we've discussed so far has focused on what you should do in order to carry out an effective and profitable social media campaign for your business but there are also some things you should <u>be sure to avoid</u> in order to be successful.**

## Top Five Common Online Networking Mistakes

Below are the top five common mistakes that businesses make when it comes to social media networking—avoid all of these.

1) Spending too much time on sites you enjoy and not fully evaluating whether or not that particular site is the most effective option for your efforts.

2) Going onto a site for "work" and then running down rabbit holes getting distracted by friends who may have posted something interesting or something which requires a response.

3) Not being able to properly define when it is more cost-effective to delegate certain social media responsibilities to someone else to handle.

4) Setting up a blog, Facebook, LinkedIn, or Twitter page and then not keeping it populated –consistency and fresh content are key.

5) Forgetting that social media is about engaging in the conversation and not just about selling.

# Chapter 9

# MLM & Power Team Networking: Good Idea or Scary Thought?

**Multi Level Marketing,** or MLM, is another term for *Direct Selling*. It can be a dual-edged sword in structured networking groups.

For starters, everybody knows somebody who started an MLM business opportunity, invested heart and soul, not to mention hard-earned cash, only to give up shortly after starting when friends and relatives threw cold water onto their dreams.

Maybe the MLM newbie didn't get the memo, business is tough. And that's true *for any business, not just MLM or network marketing.*

## Personal Perception

In many ways, network marketing is no different than any business involving sales. Let's face it, *every business* requires an element of sales. Bottom line, building a sales force is the primary task. Call it leverage; the more people selling your stuff, the better. *Better still, people who are building a sales force, or "downline" of their own to sign up everyone they know to run around and sell even more stuff.* That's where you make the big money in MLM.

And there lies the rub. There's a *personal* element to leveraging your network marketing efforts. In other words, most of the network marketing business opportunities train their people to *reach out to friends and family as the newbie's best prospects to become new associates and build the business together.*

In a traditional business, however, you hire sales people to peddle your wares rather than tap into your "warm market" of friends and family as potential business partners. Truth is, while we are all relatively numb to a sales pitch for a product, most folks still manage to nurse an inner dream of financial independence, more money than they will ever need and complete time freedom—in short, the life of their dreams. And dreams can be fragile.

Unlike a product pitch, which we brush off on a daily basis with little, if any, emotional fallout, *asking someone to be your business partner and achieve those hopes and dreams is a hot button*, a potential raw nerve forcing people to confront their own inadequacies and insecurities, especially talking to friends and family. Call it a reality check. And in today's wired world of communication overload, who needs more reality? Painful as it might be, the answer is: Lots of people! That's why MLM is so popular.

## A Rising Tide

The most recent count from the Direct Marketing Association of over 200 MLM businesses had over 15 million people involved in one network marketing company or another. And that's just in the USA alone!

Obviously, network marketing has an allure. Terms like "residual income," "home-based business," and our old buddy "leverage" are catnip for the inner tiger of any self-respecting entrepreneur. Done right, network marketing is a great way to make money and have more control over your time.

What does "done right" mean? Lots of things: prospecting, presenting and closing, to name a few.

Let's focus on the "PC" of allowing MLMers into your Power Team network. In this case however, "PC" stands for "Pros and Cons."

---

*Nathan Dominguez – BNI Arizona Executive Director:*
*"The Power of Personal Development"*

*"One of the most important things for me and network marketing is the importance of ongoing personal development and always staying fresh with renewed focus on being the best I can be. I've found that the people who are successful in network marketing understand that it is a personal development infused industry, and I really like that."*

## Pros and Cons

The best network marketers are professional inviters, charismatic people with great communication skills who know how to motivate a prospect into action.

Top MLMers are referral artists, painting compelling images each and every day of opportunity, teamwork and the rewards of financial freedom. *Properly trained to be your Bragging Buddy*, these networking whirlwinds will find a ton of money on the table for your business!

Write this down: *The MLMer has to understand and abide by the concept of Givers Gain®, helping others first and then benefitting in return.*

The problem, like any other industry group, not all MLMers get it. Overcoming the temptation to cannibalize the rest of the Power Team, hammering away at the other members to sign up for the MLM business opportunity, is no easy task. But fear not, like everything else, there is a way Power Team partners can introduce their MLM opportunity to anyone interested without alienating their best referral sources.

The best companies and representatives focus on selling their products or services – they are not in it simply for the business opportunity.

## Power Team, Not Power Prospects

For purposes of clarity on a too-often blurry concept, let's stress, like everything else, the primary goal of MLMers *is to create business for the other members of the Power Team and in return, train the group to bring referrals for their business.*

Just like every other person on the Power Team, the MLMer has to first learn to be an effective Bragging Buddy. Similarly, rather than treat the Power Team as a group of "power prospects," a good MLMer sees the Power Team as part of his or her sales force.

Yes, the sales force reciprocates, diligently on the lookout for prospects who will benefit from the MLMer's product…oh, yeah, remember the product? But the sales force *cannot be on the defensive as a prospect if they are not interested in the product or business opportunity for themselves.*

---

*Nathan Dominguez* – BNI Arizona Executive Director:
*"Don't Shoot Yourself in the Foot"*

*"Networking is all about education, and not about sales. Networking is educating our friends and family how to sell for us, and not selling to them. Unfortunately, a lot of MLM or network marketers approach networking with more of a sales mentality.*

*Building trust is the number one goal for a network marketing person trying to build a business in a structured networking group, and as we all know, trust takes time. Ultimately it is about long-term relationships.*

*I see people doing it the wrong way. They get into a networking group, jump on short, quick and easy relationships, try to sign those people up to their MLM and wonder why nobody does.*

*In a structured networking group you are shooting yourself in the foot if you try to sell or promote the business opportunity over the product or service. In a networking environment, the majority of people are there to grow a business they already have, they are not there looking for a new business.*

*On the other hand, a successful network marketer will lead with their product or service, get people interested from that angle, and inevitably some of them love what you are doing, they get to know you, like you and trust you, and decide they want to do the business, too."*

## Big Dogs – Tall Weeds

It has been said that we are the average of the five people we spend the most time with. Hang out with millionaires, chances are you've got money. Or will soon. Roll with environmental activists and it's a good bet you're passionate about saving the planet. Network with MLMers and, well, fill in the blank.

Truth is, MLM carries a stigma, particularly in networking circles. At the very least, **MLM is a dual-edged sword. And which way the blade cuts is a function of the person, NOT the business model.**

Done right, MLMers can be a tremendous value to your network. Done wrong, MLMers can burn the bridges you have worked so hard to build.

So tell us, do you want MLMers in your Power Team network?

## Take a Test

To be an effective Bragging Buddy you must believe in the value of the product or service, and also have *a strong emotional feeling the prospect will love working with your Power Team partner.*

Check yourself. *How do you feel when someone tells you that their business is "network marketing" or MLM?* Wait! Before you spit up your drink, please loosen your collar and take a deep breath. *Relax.* Now, picture on your mind's hi-def flat-screen a nice, smart and savvy MLMer who scores 100% on the following test, and take notice if a sense of calm begins to ease your troubled mind.

- Does this person represent a product or service I believe is a good value with measurable benefits to the consumer?

- Is this person more interested in what's best for the consumer rather than simply making a sale and pitching their business opportunity to everyone who fogs a mirror?

- Is this person committed to their MLM team business model, supporting their down line to generate income with useful help?

- Will this person understand that the Power Team is the sales force, not the target market?

---

*Nathan Dominguez – BNI Arizona Executive Director: "Training"*

*"The risk you take when you pass a referral to someone in a network marketing business category is this: Is this person going to try to sell the prospect on the business opportunity or is this person going to provide value to them based on their product or service?*

*One way to limit that risk is to train your referral sources on how to handle the referrals you give them. Unfortunately, I see a lot of networkers fail to do that and then get pissed off afterwards because their networking partner promoted the business opportunity to the person they were referred to, and all the person wanted was the product or service."*

## Worth the Risk?

*Clearly, referring prospects to your Power Team exposes you to the possibility of your networking partner dropping the ball and making you look bad.* That can happen with any type of business, not just MLM. Either way, nothing kills the trust you've worked so long and hard to build than a prospect doing business with one of your networking partners based on your compelling, heartfelt recommendation, only to have that referral go horribly wrong.

This does happen. Once in a blue moon circumstances beyond the control of your Power Team partner get in the way of making a good first impression. That's where communication and people skills come in. Right now let's keep our *focus on avoiding mistakes rather than cleaning up a mess.*

Power Team networking is all about quality control. If one of your networking partners proves to be more of a liability than a credit to your good name, you've got to "cut bait and start fishing" for someone new.

Even more important: before adding a new MLM business to your Power Team **make sure the person operating the business has what it takes to make you look good in the eyes of the prospects you will be sending their way.**

---

### Nathan Dominguez – BNI Arizona Executive Director:
#### "Lead With the Product"

*"At a networking conference I got to know a guy named Jeff Davidson who is a BNI Director in Miami, Florida and a successful Realtor. A friend of mine, named Jordan Adler, and I mentioned to him that my wife is a Realtor who had been using a really great follow-up system called Send Out Cards.*

*He hadn't heard of it, so we set up my laptop and showed it to him right there in the lobby of the hotel. We showed him only the product, mentioned nothing of the business opportunity. By the time we were done, he handed us his credit card and signed up just as a customer.*

*After the conference he started sending cards. A couple of months later he sent a card to his sister in Denver. She liked it so much she called him and asked him about how she could send out cards too. We upgraded him to a distributor account, did a three-way call with his sister, who signed up and started using the cards.*

*One of the cards she sent was to a friend in another network marketing company. He liked the cards a lot and immediately signed up as a distributor. Jeff's sister and her friend saw an opportunity for themselves right away. Part of the reason is because they both were introduced to it by someone they know, like and trust.*

*Now between the three of them we have a team of over 800 people thanks to leading with the product, not the opportunity, and allowing people to make a decision when the time is right for them to get into the business."*

# Chapter 10

# *Power Team Action Grid*

In Chapter 6, *Train Your Power Team*, we looked at your first face-to-face meeting with a Power Team partner. After using the Ten Key Questions to interview each other, you exchanged C2C Worksheets to focus on each other's targeted prospects, Golden Goose referral sources and how to be an effective Bragging Buddy for each other's business.

The final agenda item for your first face-to-face meeting with every Power Team partner is to work through the Power Team Action Grid together.

Illustration 10A

| *Power Team Action Grid* | | | | | | | |
|---|---|---|---|---|---|---|---|
| **Power Team Partners:** | | | | | | | |
| **Business Category:** | | | | | | | |
| **RESEARCH / PREPARATION** INSTRUCTIONS: Enter completion date for each activity listed below | | | | | | | |
| Complete 10 Key Questions | | | | | | | |
| Key Situations/Targeted Prospects | | | | | | | |
| Golden Goose Referrals | | | | | | | |
| Brag About | | | | | | | |
| Look/Listen | | | | | | | |
| **PROMOTIONAL ACTIVITY** INSTRUCTIONS: Enter completion date for each activity listed below | | | | | | | |
| To Clients | | | | | | | |
| To Co-Workers | | | | | | | |
| At Business Events | | | | | | | |
| To Potential Golden Geese | | | | | | | |
| **GROUP ACTIVITY** INSTRUCTIONS: Enter completion date for each activity listed below | | | | | | | |
| Display Business Cards | | | | | | | |
| Websites, Links & Reviews | | | | | | | |
| Combine Advertising | | | | | | | |
| Combine Efforts at Trade Shows | | | | | | | |
| Create Custom Key Situations | | | | | | | |
| Schedule a Job Tour | | | | | | | |
| Host a Workshop or Seminar | | | | | | | |
| Host a Social Event | | | | | | | |
| **REFERRAL TRACKING** INSTRUCTIONS: Enter completion date for each activity listed below | | | | | | | |
| Given/Received Inside Referrals | | | | | | | |
| Given/Received Outside Referrals | | | | | | | |
| Created a Golden Goose | | | | | | | |

© by Ivan Misner and Money on the Table Book

## Ready for Action

Write your networking partner's name and business category in the boxes at the top of the Power Team Action Grid, then in the "Research/Preparation" section mark the progress made so far in this meeting.

The list below will only be completed when you have gained enough information about your networking partner to be a consistently effective Bragging Buddy, and likely will not be finished after only one meeting.

Write your completion date on the Power Team Action Grid in the boxes for the items below.

- Targeted Prospects/Key Situations

- Golden Goose Referrals

- Product or Service Benefits to Brag About

- Target Phrases and Visual Cues to Listen and Look For

Congratulations! You have now worked your way through the Research/ Preparation stage of the Power Team Action Grid!

## Promotional Activity – Bragging Buddy

An effective Bragging Buddy tells a prospect how great you are and why the prospect should like, trust and do business with you. Let's face it, we are all inundated with print advertising and TV commercials and, in truth, most people are numb from the information overload our wired-up society dishes up 24 hours a day, seven days a week.

In contrast, a heartfelt testimonial from another person makes a deep and lasting positive impression the mass media can't touch. People want to do business with people they like and trust. It's that simple. And word-of-mouth praise from another person is the most powerful way to jumpstart the process of building trust.

The "Promotional Activity" section of the Power Team Action Grid measures your performance as a Bragging Buddy. Enter the completion date after successfully finishing each activity.

*Peter George – Marketing Coach: "Referrals and Reputations"*

*"Before I give a referral I always think about my reputation. I don't give referrals for people if I think my reputation is going to be questioned at*

*any point. There are some people, whether we are in related businesses or not, who I have no problem putting my reputation on the line with. The more comfortable I feel that way, the more referrals I give to those people."*

### Bragging to Clients

You are a personal trainer. The client wants to lose weight (Getting Healthy Key Situation) and **asks you if you recommend any meal replacement systems.** Bingo! You tell them about your Power Team partner in the nutrition business who has a fabulous line of power shakes and nutrition bars that are very effective with weight loss.

You ask the client if it would be okay for the nutritionist to call and talk about the meal replacement products. Of course, the client says "yes!"

You have just been an **order taker** for the nutritionist. The client asked for a specific product that one of your Power Team partners sells and you made the connection!

 **Power Team Tip:** *Order takers are priceless to your business! Most order takers will come from your own industry group because they will frequently be working with a client who could also use your services. order takers are a great place to start in building your network, but do not overlook businesses from the other industry groups you share a targeted prospect with.*

### From Order Taker to Connector

As a personal trainer, the people who come to you are looking to "get in shape." In addition to their own ideas on what they want or need and asking your opinion, like the meal replacement system in the example above, your clients are open to your suggestions to buy products and use services to help achieve their goals.

As a personal trainer, you are a potential Golden Goose for the other wellness professions in your Power Team.

The fact that you have a massage therapist, chiropractor, nutritional salesperson and a water purification person (or any other combination of wellness professions) on your Power Team makes you a valuable resource to your clients.

But don't stop there! You do not have to limit your networking activity to simply being an order taker, waiting for clients to ask if you "know someone who can help me...?"

Be a connector. Hand a "Getting Healthy" brochure highlighting your Health and Wellness Power Team, or your business card organizer, to the client and say, "Mrs. Jones, you've come to me as a personal trainer to help you get in shape. *Here is a group of people I work with on a regular basis who might be a good fit for us to team up with to help you achieve your goals.* These people are all very good at what they do! I know them personally and use their services myself."

---

### *Taru Fisher* – Personal Fitness: *"Power of the Business Card Book"*

*"We have a little tiny waiting area in our fitness center and I have my BNI business card book in there on a red table with other important information. I have a note on the book that says, "These are people I highly recommend and if you take a card please let us know and ask us any questions you might have about these people."*

*We work with a really neat, older couple in their 70s who come to us for strength training, so this older lady picked up the book of business cards and she pulled a bunch of cards out, came up to me, and we talked about each person. In our conversation she said they were looking to do a number of things. One was remodel their kitchen, so I referred them to our kitchen and bath remodel contractor.*

*They were also looking to redo their investments so I referred them to our financial planner. They asked about who to call when their computer went down. So I referred them to our personal computer guy. I actually had seven referrals for them."*

## Bragging For Other Targeted Prospects or Key Situations

Continuing with the personal trainer example, let's say your client mentions during one of your workouts something that has **absolutely nothing to do with getting healthy.** Maybe the client is making plans to get married. Or start a new business. Or build/remodel a home, have a baby, or are making arrangements to move into or out of town. These are the other five Key Situations that, in addition to people getting healthy, are the backbone of Power Team networking.

*"Something I do to create more referrals for the businesses I network with is at the top of our letterhead. There's a paragraph I include that says, "We pride ourselves on providing great service to our customers and we are always on the lookout for ways to make their lives easier or save money. As a result, here is a list of our strategic partners who give special offers on any number of products and services."*

*I don't put down the name of the person or company because it gives me flexibility on who I refer for any given situation. So that's part of the package I ask them to look through while I'm filling out the paperwork. That works great for me and I give a lot of referrals."*

## Bragging to Coworkers

Other people who "do what you do" face many of the same business challenges. They also have many of the same opportunities, particularly the opportunity to create referrals for products and services of your Power Team.

For example, personal trainers have an ongoing opportunity to refer their clients to massage therapists, nutritionists, chiropractors, and the other professions in the wellness industry.

The same is true for all industries. Realtors are regularly referring their clients to home inspectors, mortgage officers, insurance agents and building contractors. For jewelers, it is usually photographers, florists, caterers, and tuxedo and dress shops. You get the idea.

Whatever industry you are in, be a Bragging Buddy to other people who do what you do and leverage your networking efforts by creating Golden Goose referral sources for your Power Team. It only takes a couple of productive, new Golden Geese to make a big bottom-line difference for almost any business.

*Alina Pellicer, LMT* – *Massage Therapist: "A True Golden Goose"*

*"I have a client who is also in the wellness field and is a true Golden Goose for me. She is the nursing administrator at one of the local hospitals and she hires me every year for Nurses' Week. I come in and do chair massages. That has turned into a great group of clients.*

*I got that client from another client, a nurse at the same hospital who asked me to donate a gift certificate as a door prize they could promote to sweeten the deal and help increase attendance at their monthly* meeting. I thought, sure, I'd love to get another client in the medical field, so I donated the gift certificate and the person who won was the head of the Nurse's Department!

She's really great and has turned into a real promoter of my business. In fact, she introduced me to the nursing administrator at another local hospital. You just never know how one thing can lead to another. Not only that, she's planning to do the same thing with chair massages for the doctors just like what she did for the nurses, so we'll see what happens!"

## Bragging at Business Events

Trade shows, mixers, conferences, seminars and business workshops of any type are a great environment to create Golden Goose referral sources. If possible, go to the event with a Power Team partner and brag about them as you both meet people who might be their prospect as a customer/client or Golden Goose. That's right, sing your networking partner's praises right there as they stand back and smile! And let them do the same for you.

## Bragging Buddy Tips

### 1) Use the Key Situation Flyers or a Business Card Organizer

The Key Situation Flyers (visit www.moneyonthetablebook.com) and business card organizers are very effective tools for *uncovering additional needs the prospect isn't thinking about at the moment.* As a result, you create multiple referrals, and in many cases future referrals for your Power Team.

---

*James Hamilton* –*ADT Security Systems:*
*"Business Cards, Babies and Burglar Alarms"*

*"A life insurance agent gave me a referral for a young couple who were expecting a baby. They decided to move out of Manhattan and bought a home in northern New Jersey. While they were doing the paperwork for the life insurance, he let his clients go through his business card holder with his networking partners' cards and of course, my card was in there.*

*The husband went through the cards and said, "Here are two things we need, Honey, baby furniture and a burglar alarm system." He sends those great referrals because he systematically promotes me and our entire network as part of his process."*

## 2) Help the Prospect to "Like and Trust" Your Power Team Partner

*Brag about the quality of the person in addition to the quality of the product or service.* Why does your Power Team partner love what they do?

Talk about your experience or a third-party testimonial – have a success story to tell! What separates your Power Team partner from the competition?

---

### *Bill Coniam* – *25th Street Automotive: "Grandson as Collateral"*

*"What I've learned from my BNI Chapter is that referral marketing is about relationships. It takes time to build that relationship. I find that our customers or our networking contacts, once they know us, refer people to us because of that trust.*

*The trust level can be amazing. Years ago, a customer came in and "Oops," they didn't have money on them to pay the bill. They left their grandson as collateral and went to get their money. That's the kind of trust they have in their local car guy!"*

## 3) Get the Prospect's Contact Information

The cliché is true; "the fortune is in the follow up!" Position your Power Team to follow up with prospects by getting their contact info and you will greatly increase the referral to business ratio!

---

### *Hazel Walker* – *BNI and Referral Institute: "Referral Standards"*

*"If all I did was hand a prospect a business card from one of my networking partners, it wouldn't be a referral. It would be a lead. It would be at a very low level and I don't do that. Here's why: How I give referrals to other people is how I'm training them to give referrals to me. So if all I'm doing is handing out cards and saying "Call this person," that's all they are going to do for me.*

*I will not accept that level of a referral. The minimum level referral I will accept is a face-to-face introduction, or at least a phone introduction. So if that is what I want to receive, that's how I give. I go to great lengths to give a testimonial.*

*One of my referral partners is a sales trainer named Aaron. When I refer Aaron, I give a testimonial about his sales training program, I talk about the results I've had using the program and then I set up a time* when I can get both of them together for a phone call, and then I do a three-way phone call. I take the extra effort to make it happen.

Aaron is a great referral partner for me. He sends me a lot of business because his target market and my target are absolutely identical."

### 4) Be Enthusiastic!

The power of heightened, positive energy is not to be underestimated. Crank up the volume on your Bragging Buddy efforts and you will become a networking powerhouse!

---

*Hazel Walker* – BNI and Referral Institute:
*"Enthusiasm and Making a Difference"*

*"I think enthusiasm is very important as long as it's not over-the-top. We've all met that person who is a little too enthusiastic and wears you out. But having a positive attitude, a good smile, being enthusiastic about helping people is vital to a good network. When you are contributing to other people in a way that makes a difference in their life, it creates a life for you, too."*

The more people from your Power Team strategically working together, the **greater the number and quality of money-making referrals generated.**

The Group Activity section of the Power Team Action Grid measures your performance as a Power Team. Enter the completion date into the boxes after successfully finishing each activity.

## Business Card Displays

Business card displays are terrific indicators of a Power Team's vitality.

Add up the number of businesses on your Power Team operating out of a fixed location with good foot traffic. Businesses like the printer, florist, jeweler, auto shop, furniture sales, insurance or real estate office and chiropractor or massage therapist's office.

Now count how many of these fixed location businesses have a prominent, professional looking business card display for their Power Team and calculate the percentage.

**Bottom line**: The higher the percentages of businesses with a prominent Power Team business card display, the healthier the group.

## Websites, Links and Reviews

Your Power Team may choose to create a website promoting your networking group and all the individual members. At a minimum, exchange links to as many of your Power Team partners' websites as possible.

Another effective way to build each other's business online is to write reviews and give glowing satisfaction ratings for each other on websites like Yahoo, Google, Bing, and Merchant's Circle among many others.

## Combine Advertising

Does your business advertise? If so, consider partnering up with your Power Team partners who also advertise to increase exposure and lower costs. Combined Power Team advertising efforts in the newspaper, radio, television and Internet can lead to cross-over business that works in everybody's favor.

## Trade Shows

Your Power Team might decide to join forces for a booth at a trade show. In some cases, your group may actually create a "show," conference or seminar for a particular target market to generate a buzz around the Power Team's products and services. Examples include a bridal and wedding show, home remodel expo, or pet health and training workshop to name a few.

## Custom Key Situations

Some Power Teams have members who "think outside the box." Creative, free-thinking entrepreneurs who are able to identify a targeted prospect for a cross-section of industry groups, which nobody else has identified. And as a result, finds new money on the table for the group.

For example, let's say the nutritionist in the group is readying sales efforts for the allergy season. People with allergies are a great referral for the nutritionist because proper nutrition bolsters a person's immune system with vitamins and minerals to relieve the sniffing, sneezing and coughing from allergies.

During a face-to-face meeting with the air conditioning person on the Power Team, the nutritionist learns that the air conditioning company gets a lot of calls from people with allergies. Usually, people are concerned about the air filters, ducts and overall air quality in their home as a contributor to their sneezing, wheezing, itchy eyes and overall discomfort.

Bingo: the nutritionist and air conditioning company just uncovered a Key Situation they can both capitalize on!

The nutritionist then realizes that many of the other businesses on the Power Team, particularly the Property Services and Wellness Contact Spheres, also deal with people who either have allergies or other respiratory issues on a regular basis.

In this way, the "Allergy" Power Team is born!

Now when any Power Team partner comes across a prospect with allergies, he or she creates referrals by simply saying, "I network with a group of local businesses that work together to help people with allergies. Here's a flyer that shows what they do. I've referred lots of people to this group and have heard nothing but great things about how they've helped people get over their allergies! Please let me know if you would like the contact information for any of these businesses."

Every business category has at least one, and usually more, custom Key Situations that can be the focal point for a Power Team. Have fun brainstorming!

---

### Patrick Finley – *Art Promotional Services, LLC: "Power Team Meeting"*

*"When our Power Team gets together each month we talk about three people we've recently closed sales with. Then everyone talks about three specific people we want to meet or we are trying to get to and we all kick around ideas for a few minutes. To close out the last part of the meeting, we bring in a "Spotlight" member from our networking group. If someone has specific questions for us or needs some marketing advice, whether it's promotional, advertising or social media, whatever, they have 20 minutes or so to sit there and pick our brains.*

*The week before the meeting, we send out an email with a few questions about how things are going now, their best referrals, how they are getting those, are they cold calling, what are they doing right now to market their business? That helps us come up with some questions for them, so it's a good back-and-forth.*

*We have 20 minutes dedicated to that, but most of the time 20 minutes turns into an hour. We love sitting there and talking about this stuff, and we come up with some great ideas that help our other networking partners make more money, and in turn, they tell other people about how we've helped them!"*

## Job Tour

Taking an hour or two as a group to visit the job site of other networking partners makes you a much more effective Bragging Buddy.

The painting contractor could take the group on a tour of current and recently completed jobs. Or the Realtor offers a tour of her current listings. An attorney could invite the group to attend a trial he is litigating or an auto repair business could hold an open house and tour of the facilities.

Whatever the business, there is usually a way to invite your networking partners to a view behind the scenes of your operation, and in the process, become a much more authoritative Bragging Buddy as they tell the world about you.

## Host a Workshop or Seminar

*Sam Schwartz* – BNI National and Executive Director:
*"Power Team Super Group"*

*"I have a group of businesses that actually worked so well together they formed a new company. All of the businesses had a common target market: CEOs of companies with annual sales of over one million dollars. One was a CEO for hire, another does branding and marketing, another ran mastermind groups, another did financing, there was a sales coach and a few other related categories.*

*They had a flyer made and built collateral materials as a group. When any one of them would go to meet a CEO they would bring the entire team. They would put the CEO in the center and ask, "How can we help you?" They did all of their marketing as a team and have built a very successful business together.*

*They would do seminars together. Each of the people in the network would invite a CEO or two and then each of the networkers would give a ten to fifteen minute short presentation on a snapshot of what they do related to the specific topic. The focus was never to sell but to educate about what they do and as a result, they almost always got new clients."*

## Social Event

Getting the group together for a meal at a restaurant, or a barbecue at a local park or someone's home is a great way to build rapport with your networking partners and create new referrals from other guests in attendance.

### *James Hamilton* – ADT Security Systems:
*"The Architect, Soirée and Museum"*

*"There is a content provider in my BNI Chapter whose wife is an architect. After I put in a burglar alarm and fire detection system in their house, the wife spoke to a friend about the system. The friend's boss is one of the curators at the Museum of Modern Art.*

*The architect and content provider had a soirée where I met the curator. It turns out they are already protected by our products, but directly through the corporation as opposed to through us as a local dealer. He asked me about the differences between going through us or direct and I told him the advantages and disadvantages. Bottom line is that we can offer better pricing, so he asked me to join him at the next board meeting to give the board of directors a rundown on what I just told him.*

*I went to the board meeting and they asked me to write up a proposal. I wrote it up then didn't hear back from them. I followed up and they said they still hadn't made a decision, so I figured nothing is going to come out of this.*

*Shortly after that I got a phone call, "When can you begin the installation?" So they made the switch from corporate to us as the local dealer. We got the Museum of Modern Art as a client as the result of a content provider's wife who is an architect who knows the curator of the museum! That was a very juicy job for us and it keeps on going. The installation and upgrades totaled well over $150,000 of business for us."*

### *Sam Schwartz* – BNI National and Executive Director:
*"Playing the Float: Power Team Meeting on a Boat "*

*"I have an attorney named Charlie in one of my networking groups who specializes in providing financing to small businesses who need to lease expensive equipment. Charlie owns a boat and he put together a Power Team meeting that required his networking partners to bring two or three of their top clients, and he decided to do it on the boat.*

*The guests had no idea of the networking that was planned. They were just invited for a fun day on the boat. The beauty of this is that no one could get off the boat! The Power Team agreed in advance that the goal was not to sell, but to network, make introductions and maybe provide some information that may be helpful for future networking. The boat trip worked out great and I know for a fact that a lot of business took place as a result."*

## Referral Tracking

The final application of the Power Team Action Grid is to track referrals. Be sure to keep a running tally of the referrals you give and receive.

You should have the name and business category of each Power Team partner across the top of the Power Team Action Grid (use as many sheets as you need).

Mark the Inside, Outside and Golden Goose referrals with a "G" if you were the Giver or "R" if you were the Recipient.

Track the referral activity on an ongoing basis and review the results during face-to-face meetings. Power Team partners who are not passing referrals back and forth need to refocus on their Key Situations, targeted prospects and Bragging Buddy activities.

---

### Tiffanie Kellog  – TiffaniKellog.com: "Why Power Teams Fail"

*"One of the things that we always look at is why Power Teams fail. One reason that is high up on the list is that a lot of people who think they are on a Power Team aren't because they don't share the same target market. Others have lack of motivation and accountability. A lot of people don't start off with seeing the value of putting the time or energy into developing the Power Team."*

---

### Sam Schwartz – BNI National and Executive Director:
"BNI, The Accountant and the $80,000 Chair"

*"An accountant in one of my BNI Chapters went to a networking meeting on April 15th, and the other members were surprised to see him there on tax day. During his sales manager minute he held up his chair and asked the group, "How much do you think this chair is worth?"*

Somebody said, "One hundred dollars." Another said, "A thousand dollars." The CPA said, "Not even close. This chair is worth $80,000! That's how much I made in the past twelve months from my involvement in this networking group. How do I know? I'm an accountant and I keep track. That's why even though today is tax day, I'm here to protect my seat and the value it brings to my business!"

**Chapter 11**

# *Build Your Power Team*

How big should the Power Team be? The answer will depend on you, your business and the commitment of the people on your team.

Two businesses, working strategically together, are capable of creating a huge referral relationship for each other as a Power Team. A chiropractor and massage therapist, Realtor and mortgage lender, insurance and security system sales, and event planner and caterer are a few obvious examples. Most businesses however will begin seeing the results with a group that includes **at least four** *productive* **networking partners from their own industry, and another four from different industries that also share the same targeted prospects.**

The sky is the limit. Studies done in BNI show when the size of the group doubles, the number of referrals triple! How much money on the table are you looking for?

Later in the chapter we'll listen to the language of inviting. Let's start now looking at where to find your Power Team partners.

## *Start With Your Own Contact Sphere*

Look at the Contact Sphere illustration 3A in Chapter 3 and take inventory of the people and business categories you currently network with from your own Contact Sphere.

 **Power Team Building Tip** *Using the Contact Sphere as a guide, write the names of your current networking partners (next to their business category) who are already exchanging referrals as a Power Team. Any open categories are potential Golden Goose referral sources for your business.*

*Now look at the Connector to Creator (C2C) Worksheet and take inventory of the Golden Goose business categories for your best Key Situations. These are other businesses that may be from different industry groups, but also share your same targeted prospects market. Are you networking with them?*

## From Start to Finish

If you are starting from scratch, fine. Sharpen your pencil and let's get busy! You are officially declared the Power Team Leader, and Chapter 12 was written just for you.

If you already belong to a networking group, the process will be a little different, but the underlying principles of leadership and team building are the same.

Let's say that you already belong to a networking group and are in the carpet cleaning business. You sit down with the licensed handyman from your group. In fact, let's say you and the handyman are the only two business categories from the Property Services Contact Sphere currently in your networking group. All the other Property Services categories are unfilled or "Open."

Brainstorm with your networking partner on whom the two of you already know in the open categories. Remember, you are looking for people who are good at what they do and are looking to build their business.

## Beyond the Industry

In Chapters 13 through 18 we go through each of the six Contact Spheres in detail, itemizing how each business category can do tons of business in each Key Situation. Some will be obvious, others less common but potentially even more powerful.

Either way, in addition to your own Contact Sphere, networking together with businesses outside your industry that also share your targeted prospects greatly expands your network and dramatically increases the numbers of referrals you can give and receive. While members of the same industry can be prolific order taker and connector referral sources, they often feed from the same client pool. Adding members of the other industries brings an essential element to the Power Team, a greater variety of fresh contacts.

## Power of Intention + Action

**Knowing which business categories you are looking for** is the essential first element of building your Power Team. Keeping those business categories top-of-mind and at the forefront of conversations will create opportunities to bring the right people, in the right businesses, into your network.

Now what?

After completing this book, you will be fully prepared to approach people in the business categories you need. But rather than keep you at the edge of your seat, all dressed up and nowhere to go, let's dive into the prospecting process and have some fun.

## Five-Way Street

Here are five ways to prospect for new Power Team members:

1) Talk to business people you already know

2) Talk to business people you are referred to by people you already know

3) "Do the Mingle" – Get out and about, talk to new people wherever you are

4) The "Oh, by the way…" technique to turn any phone call into a team-building event

5) Cold Call – Pick up the phone and call people you don't know in the business categories you are looking for

## Dialing for Dollars

Let's watch a pro in action. Manny Goodbuys, a Realtor in the early stages of building his Power Team is on the telephone. He's recruiting his favorite mortgage broker, Seymour Dollars. Remember, these are **people who already know each other**.

*"Hi, Seymour, its Manny over at the Real Estate Store! Do you have a moment for me? Great – Seymour, whenever you and I work together you always do a great job with the people I've sent to you for a loan. Here's the deal, I'm putting together a networking group that only allows one person per profession. I would like to put you in the running to be the group's mortgage expert. Are you interested?"*

If Seymour says yes, Manny and Seymour will schedule a time to meet one-on-one in the next 48 hours to talk in greater detail. We will focus on what to say during that first meeting later in Chapter 12, *Notes to the Power Team Leader*.

If Manny's group was already established, he would invite Seymour to be his guest at the regularly scheduled networking meeting. Either way, if the answer is no, Manny plans to ask Seymour who he knows in the mortgage business who is good at what they do and _is_ looking to grow their business.

Three things can happen. A "fear of loss" could kick in for Seymour and he suddenly becomes interested in the Power Team because he doesn't want to pass on an opportunity that winds up making money for someone else. If not, Seymour either gives Manny the contact information for another mortgage officer or he doesn't. Whatever the outcome, the odds are two-out-of-three Manny will end the call with a new prospect for the Power Team.

## Calling People You Were Referred To

In a perfect world, anyone who gives you the name and contact information for someone he or she thinks would be a good fit for your Power Team should call the prospect first, letting the prospect know who you are and why you will be calling. But as we know, it is not a perfect world.

With that in mind, the following example works even when the prospect does not get an introduction call from the person who connected you. However, in the example below we took the liberty of adding a couple of business categories to the network's roster, demonstrating the magnetic attraction of a functioning Power Team.

- Hi, is this Debbie the general contractor?

- Debbie, my name is Manny Goodbuys, I'm a Realtor and I got your name and number from my mortgage guy, Seymour Dollars.

- I'm part of a networking group and we are looking for a general contractor to refer our clients to and Seymour tells me that you are very good at what you do.

- Are you looking for more business?

- Would referrals from other local businesses be of interest to you?

- _If NO:_ Who do you know in your business who is looking to make more money?

- _If YES:_ I have _____ people on my sales team, including a licensed handyman and an air conditioning company. The handyman has a great business but he's always coming across jobs that are too big and he needs a general contractor to refer to. Same with the A/C guy. They install new systems and repair old systems and are talking to people on a daily basis about major home renovations that they of course don't do. And that's just two of the people on my Power Team.

- Would you be interested in getting together with me so I can show you the Power Team system I'm using to generate referrals for myself and my partners?

- If this sounds interesting, I would like to introduce you to my networking partners.

## Do the "Mingle"

For most people, meeting other people face-to-face is the easiest, most productive way to prospect for their Power Team.

Opportunity is everywhere. Business functions such as Chamber of Commerce events or community service groups like the Rotary or Optimists, provide excellent opportunities to find Power Team prospects. Same with any group or club. Churches, temples, local softball or bowling leagues, art and performance guilds, Toastmasters, Big Brothers/Big Sisters, historical preservation societies…the list is endless.

## Prospect at Events or Throughout the Day

Trade shows can be very productive. From home improvement fairs and bridal expos to car shows and health and wellness events, be sure to prospect the vendors who represent businesses you are looking for. Ask them who else they know in the business categories you seek.

Finally, you can find Power Team prospects randomly as you go about your normal daily activities at places like the grocery store, the waiting room of a doctor's office or chatting with neighbors while walking the dog.

## Meeting People Face-to-Face

Like it or not, meeting people face-to-face involves small talk. And the *more you get people to talk about who they are and what they do*, the more interesting *you* become to them. In fact, the other person will consider you a great conversationalist. Face it, people love talking about themselves!

The trick to upgrading small talk and idle chatter into Power Team prospecting is discovering if the prospect, or someone they know, is in a business category you are seeking to build your network.

After exchanging basic pleasantries, ask people about what they do. If they are in a business category your Power Team is looking for, ask a few more questions to determine if they might be someone with whom you would like to network.

If you like what you see and hear, tell them about your Power Team. If they show an interest, invite them to your next networking meeting or if you are starting the group from scratch, schedule an appointment for the interview. See Chapter 12, *Notes to the Power Team Leader* for details.

If the person is *not* in a business you want to add, salvage the prospecting effort by asking for a business category you *are* looking for, "Who do you know in the _____ business? Someone who is good at what they do and looking for more business?"

## The "Oh, by the Way..." Technique

Another great opportunity to find Power Team prospects comes at the end of every business phone call you make. Simply ask the person you are speaking with whom they know in a particular business category.

Example: *"Oh, by the way, before I hang up, do you know someone in the _____ business who is good at what they do and looking for more business?"* You will be amazed at the results!

In the next Chapter, *Notes to the Power Team Leader,* we get into the details of contacting the people you've identified in the open business categories to invite them to take a look at your Power Team network as a way to help build their business.

## Cold Calls

Working together, you and your ever-increasing circle of Power Team partners should be able to find most, or all of the businesses you need through your existing connections and the people your collective connections know.

But after you have contacted all the people you already know in all six Contact Spheres, as well as those you continue to meet at sushi bars and mixers or to whom you were referred by someone you know, you may find the need to accelerate the Power Team's development by reaching out to businesses in open categories that have *no known connection to you or the other Power Team partners*.

Yes, that's right – the time has come for COLD CALLING!

Question: Where do we find prospects?

Answer: On the telephone!

The most obvious source of companies in the specific open categories you are targeting is the Internet and the Yellow Pages. Viewed from a targeted prospect perspective, these incredibly valuable and free reference tools provide an abundance of information on people in any business category you can imagine.

And then you've got newspapers, local magazines, coupon mailers, community bulletin boards, vehicle signs, and local billboards, as just a few places to look for business people interested in growing their business.

Here's an outline for a cold call:

- "Hello, is this Linda the caterer?"

- Hi Linda, My name is _____ and I'm part of a networking group that is looking for a caterer to refer our clients to.

- Linda, I found your catering business on the Internet. May I ask you a question? Would building your business with referrals from other local businesses be of interest to you?

- *If NO*: Who do you know in your business who is looking to make more money?

- *If YES*: I would like to introduce you to my networking partners – people who I pass referrals with every week, people who might be able to help build your business.

- Would you be interested in getting together with me so I can show you the Power Team system I'm using to generate referrals for myself and my networking partners?

 **Time Management Tip:** *The most time efficient way to jump-start your Power Team in this early developmental stage is to block out an hour a day to make calls. Maintain the one-hour-a-day regimen until your group has reached a critical mass of networking connections that will synergize into massive referral volume!*

## Goals for Prospecting New People

If you are building your Power Team from scratch and do not have an ongoing scheduled meeting, your first goal is to sit down and talk face-to-face to Power Team prospects. Whether meeting people for the first time, who were referred to you by someone you already know, or someone you met at a sushi bar or from a cold call, understand that *your goal is to get together with the prospect for an interview to see if that person is a good fit for your group.*

If so, then it is time to outline the Power Team program and invite them to submit an application for membership. More on that in Chapter 12, *Notes to the Power Team Leader – You!*

If you belong to a structured networking group with a regularly scheduled meeting, your goal at this point is to simply invite the prospect to visit your meeting and see the Power Team in action firsthand.

## Invite to Visit NOT Join

Here are a few basic tips to keep in mind when talking about structured Power Team meetings to **prospects you have not met:**

- Avoid creating obstacles that get in the way of a prospect attending your networking meeting as a visitor. Top of the list, suggesting they join your group. Trust us, it's counterproductive!

  To a potential visitor, the suggestion of joining your group triggers questions of "How much does it cost to join?" and "What's the commitment?" Not good for your success ratio! Plus, you haven't performed due diligence yet and don't know if you even want them in your group!

Inviting people to *visit* your networking meeting is a good thing. Statistics show that the average visitor to a structured networking meeting with an average size of 20 people will spend thousands of dollars and create a long-term networking relationship with one or more members even if they never join the group!

Let's repeat: *Invite prospects to meet with you, not join your group. Your job is to get the prospect to the networking table.* If joining is a good idea, the prospect will see it on their own.

- When inviting, *tell the prospect about how great the networking group is for your business and that you would love for them to see how it works.*

- Tell the prospect about other business categories and people in the group who would likely be a good connection based on common targeted prospects in the Six Key Situations.

For example, a prospect in the home inspection business would be interested to meet the Realtor, as well as the mortgage and insurance people in the group. A photographer would love to be introduced to your florist, caterer and event planner.

- If your Power Team has a regularly scheduled meeting, ask the prospect to **bring a stack of business cards and be ready to connect with a room full of your networking partners**, people who <u>might</u> become a source of referrals.

- When inviting someone to a structured networking meeting, let the prospect know that there **is no cost or obligation to visit, other than maybe a room or meal charge if you have one.** Most structured networking groups allow visitors to sit in on two meetings and then ask the newbie to either submit an application for membership or quit freeloading.

- **Final Point:** Be sure NOT to invite anyone to visit your group who is a potential competitor of a current Power Team member. If necessary, check with your Power Team partner for feedback on whether or not a conflict exists before extending an invitation rather than step on toes and slip backwards on the confidence curve.

Good news! Everyone can be successful prospecting for new Power Team partners. Keep it simple and you'll do fine.

## More Than What You Say, It's How You Say It

**Power Team Prospecting Tip:** *Be excited, show enthusiasm and speak from firsthand experience. What do you enjoy most about your Power Team? Talk about how your networking group has benefited you and your business. What business categories might be natural networking partners for the visitor?*

*If you genuinely feel great about your group, the person you are talking with will feel it too. And like it or not, we make decisions based on emotion. Be smart. Tap into your positive feelings. Use your emotional energy to direct that quirky thing called "human nature" to your advantage.*

# Chapter 12

# *Notes to the Power Team Leader – You!*

Ultimately, we are all leaders of our own Power Team. You may already be part of an internationally chartered, structured networking group with a leader who runs the regularly scheduled meeting. Or maybe you've been asked to join an informal, less-structured networking group that is not part of a larger organization but that nonetheless has a leadership structure already in place. You may even be building your own Power Team from scratch, sharing your Givers Gain® vision with other business people, taking action as the catalyst for an ongoing stream of money-making referrals.

This chapter is geared to the visionary, the true entrepreneur who sees money on the table and is driven to start and build a team of like-minded business professionals.

Whatever the scenario, the greater your ability to provide leadership by example, the greater benefit you will receive from networking. Bottom line: Take ownership of your network and see yourself as the leader of your own Power Team regardless of how your networking group is structured.

## *Leader's Role and Responsibilities*

Let's start with the basics. As Power Team Leader, you have *five areas of responsibility*:

1) **Selecting Members** Quality control starts with the people you allow into your Power Team.

2) **Training** Guide new networking partners through this book and the online training at www.moneyonthetablebook.com.

3) **Tracking** Monitor your Power Team activity for minimum performance standards. As leader, you set the standards.

4) **Standards Enforcement and Conflict Resolution** Power Team members who fail to perform up to minimum standards should be given an opportunity to improve performance or be removed from the team, with their business category then opened to new applicants. Conflicts between Power Team members must be resolved by the Power Team leader.

5) **Leadership** Set the example with a positive and supportive attitude, a diligent and thoughtful networking effort, as well as frequent face-to-face contact.

## Selecting Members

When you begin building your Power Team, fast is good, but not too fast. **Follow your intuition when you meet people.**

Power Team networking works best when all the people involved like and trust each other. In Chapters 13 through 18, we turbo-charge the Power Team process so you can immediately begin referring business back and forth.

Right now, however, we need to focus on the very serious business of picking the right people for your Power Team.

## Ten Key Qualities to Look For

Networkers come in all shapes and sizes. From grizzled veterans of 25+ years or more in business with an extensive network of contacts, to bright-eyed college grads just starting out and looking to make connections, there is a wide variety of people to choose from when filling your open categories.

In addition to "years of experience," "current network of contacts" and "available time, energy and commitment," Power Team prospects vary in a number of other ways.

Two primary categories are physical characteristics, such as age, gender, and ethnicity; as well as personality traits including business philosophy, communication skills and reliability.

The more diversity of the physical characteristics on your team, the better. A cross-section of demographics will create access to a much wider network for the group than a "men's only" or "women's only" Power Team, or any other group built exclusively around similar ages, ethnic background or other physical characteristics.

Not true for the personality traits. There are various types of people who will cause problems for your Power Team. It is absolutely imperative that you put together a group of like-minded people who can work well together with the same philosophy toward a common goal.

Search for people who:

1) Want to build a business actively with word-of-mouth networking rather than those who passively run advertising and wait for the phone to ring

2) Understand that business is about relationships with other business people

3) Show integrity, with a good reputation in the local community

4) Sell quality and service, NOT lowest price

5) Have businesses that demand continuous, ongoing growth

6) Are qualified, and if needed, licensed to perform their service or sell their product

7) Are enthusiastic and enjoyable to be around

8) Have connections to other businesses, prospects and influential people in the community

9) Enjoy helping others

10) Are committed to building other businesses on the Power Team with the understanding they will be compensated in turn by the Power Team helping build *their* business

## Ten Key Questions

The Ten Key Questions we covered in Chapter 6, *Train the Power Team*, can also be used face-to-face to prospect or interview someone for the Power Team:

1) How did you get started in your business?

2) What do you enjoy most about what you do?

3) What separates you and/or your company from the competition?

4) What advice would you give someone starting out in your business?

5) What are the coming trends in your business or industry?

6) What strategies have you found to be the most effective in promoting your business?

7) If there was anything about your business or industry that you could change what would it be?

8) What is the next big event coming up for you?

9) What is your biggest challenge at the moment?

10) How would I recognize a good prospect for your business?

 **Power Team Prospecting Tip:** *If you know the Six Key Situations well enough, you can help prospects by talking about their business and which targeted prospects have money on the table for them. Further, you can explain how you and the rest of the Power Team can find those types of referrals and create business for them.*

## Outlining Your Power Team Plan

After asking a prospect a series of questions, you will have a sense of whether or not you want the prospect on your team. If you get a good feeling about the prospect and would like to see him or her join your ranks, it's important to get a commitment.

Before a prospect can make that commitment, he or she has to know *what* that commitment is. Everybody likes the sound of making more money and getting referrals from other local businesses, but what's the catch? What are they going to be required to do in order to join the Power Team?

The prospect already knows from your initial contact that you are building a networking group limited to one person per profession. So far, so good. Now the prospect needs to know the details to make a decision about getting involved.

The easiest way to explain the Power Team plan in quick, easy terms and capture their imagination is to let the *Introduction to Money on the Table* brochure (www.moneyonthetablebook.com) do the heavy lifting for you.

Give the prospect the brochure after you've asked enough questions to determine if you would like to go further in exploring the prospect as a potential Power Team partner.

## Introduction to Money on the Table Brochure

Here's a sample dialogue to explain the Power Team process using the *Introduction to Money on the Table* brochure. Put things in your own words, but keep it simple and let the brochure do the work.

"This panel *Time (and Energy) is Money* briefly explains the concept that our ability to create business for someone else will result in business coming back to us if we train our networking partners properly. In other words, having a Power Team is like having a sales force, but instead of paying the sales force with cash, the team is compensated with the money-making referrals you send.

The *Power Team Example* on the left and inside center panels is a good illustration of a Power Team at work. You can see how a Power Team jeweler creates many referrals, not only for related businesses like photographers and caterers, but also for non-related businesses such as financial planning and a massage therapist, which are not referrals you would usually connect to an engagement ring purchase. That's money on the table currently falling through the cracks.

We show you which Key Situations to look for to create business for your Power Team partners and, in turn, you show them how to find the targeted prospects and Key Situations your business thrives on!

The inside right panel, *Six Key Situations* simply lists the top six common, everyday situations the Power Team is trained to recognize and convert into money-making referrals.

The back panel, *Join My Power Team*, is an outline of how the Power Team works and your commitment to the team.

You and I will have three *Orientation Meetings*, of about two hours each, where I will give you all the networking tools you need to start generating referrals for the other members of the team, as well as showing the team how to generate referrals for you.

Here is a *current roster of the people and businesses we are already networking with*. We will be ready to pass referrals to each other after the first meeting. The next orientation session will focus on a strategic plan to combine our efforts with the rest of the Power Team. How much activity, time and effort you put into it is up to you.

At the same time, *we track performance and have minimum standards.* Each Power Team partner is required to:

1) Send one email a week with an update of "What type of client I am looking for this week" to the rest of the Power Team.

2) Do at least one face-to-face meeting a week with another Power Team partner.

3) Actively generate at least three referrals a month for the Power Team.

**NOTE:** The performance standards above are examples. Set your own performance standards for your Power Team.

After going through the explanation above, ask the prospect if they are interested in joining your Power Team.

If interested, give him or her a membership application so you can check references, etc., before inviting the prospect into the group.

## *Orientation Training*

After a successful interview, your job is to help your new Power Team partner get the most out of the *Orientation Training*. The Power Team leader focuses on answering questions, brainstorming ideas and facilitating networking activity. The leader meets three times with the new member to complete the Training: Initial Orientation, Follow Up and Initial Face-to-Face Meeting.

### *Initial Orientation*

The *Initial Orientation* helps new Power Team partners become productive as soon as possible.

Be sure to schedule the meeting for a quiet location with no distractions and bring the following materials:

1) A copy of this book to give to the new member

2) The *Introduction to Money on the Table* brochure

3) Current roster of the Power Team members with contact information.

Remind the new Power Team partner of his or her responsibility to the performance standards you've set for your group.

Instruct the new member to read Chapters 1-7 of *Money on the Table,* and be prepared to discuss what they've read next time you meet.

After the Initial Orientation, schedule the *Follow Up Orientation* to create the member's *Connector to Creator Worksheet,* as well as to answer any questions they may have about the Power Team process.

## Follow Up

Based on what they've read in the first seven chapters of this book, new members will be focused on which Contact Sphere they belong to and which Key Situations work best for their businesses.

Follow this outline for your Follow Up Meeting:

1) Start by reviewing the terms and concepts in Chapter Three and answer any questions.

2) Review and customize the **Connector to Creator** ("C2C") Worksheet.

   a) Review each Key Situation for a connection to the new member's targeted prospects one at a time.

   b) Once a Key Situation clicks as a viable trigger to recognize a targeted prospect, fill in the blanks for Golden Goose referral sources, as well as the Brag About and Look and Listen For sections.

   c) Introduce the current Power Team members in the Golden Goose business categories for each targeted prospect.

   d) Brainstorm and make a list of people you *already know* in the currently open Golden Goose business categories to contact.

   e) Review the *Brag About* bullet points. Look for specific connection to the targeted prospect. "What do you want us to say to prospects that will help them like you, trust you, and want to do business with you?"

   f) Review the *Listen and Look For* target phrases and visual cues. Any new ideas?

   g) Review the **Key Situation Flyers** (www.moneyonthetablebook.com) that specifically relate to the new member's business. Introduce the current Power Team members listed in the flyer using the current Power Team Roster.

Confident that the new member has a clear understanding of the material covered, instruct them to complete the rest of this book, and when completed, schedule the Initial Face-to-Face Meeting.

## First Face-to-Face With the Leader

All new Power Team partners should have their first regular face-to-face meeting with the Power Team Leader to complete the three-part orientation before meeting the other members. In addition to the valuable exchange of information that happens during any first face-to-face, the Power Team Leader can give the new member an advanced training or final tune-up on how to use the Ten Key Questions and C2C Worksheets for maximum effectiveness. Refer to Chapter 6, *Train the Power Team* for more information.

The underlying concept of the Power Team system is to create word-of-mouth referrals for your networking partners. After all, you know who their targeted prospects are, and you also know how to give a compelling testimonial for your networking partner.

Now we simply need to systematically make the Power Team visible as we go about our business with our networking radar on alert for the targeted prospects, Key Situations and Golden Goose referrals our Power Team partners are looking for.

## Performance Tracking

As the leader, you make the rules. How often will your group meet? What format will the meeting use? How many referrals does a member need to give? The list goes on.

Whatever criteria you create, it is your responsibility to keep track of, or at least assign someone to keep track of, each member's performance and when appropriate, take proactive action to increase your Power Team's performance.

---

*Mike Roberts* – BNI Executive Director:
*"Measuring Results, Insurance and Security Systems"*

*"I met with two individuals who are members of a Power Team, Bill is a property and casualty insurance agent and John sells home security systems. They formed a Power Team to create more business for each other, and were keeping track of the referrals they were creating, but for some reason it wasn't producing the results they wanted, so they contacted me."*

I asked them a few questions about what they were currently doing, which really amounted to very little other than meeting together twice a month and trying extra hard to find more referrals for each other, but there was no real plan or strategy.

So I asked a few more questions. "Bill, how many of your clients would save money on their homeowner's insurance if they had a home security system?" He told me that they would all qualify for a discount.

Then I asked him how many of his clients do not have a security system and he said he didn't know. I pointed out that these people would be great prospects for John, and of course, he agreed. He also said that he already had this information in his records.

I turned to John and asked him about what Bill should say to these people. After all, if John doesn't teach Bill what to say, and actually come up with a strategy to work together on this, nothing will happen.

At that point I reminded them that a Power Team needs to work both ways, and I asked John, "How many of your clients are paying too much for insurance?" and he said he didn't know.

Ultimately we came up with a strategy where John systematically contacted all of his clients to check in and see how the security system was working and then also go through a short script to promote Bill's business, saying something like, "I have a networking partner who does property and casualty insurance and he may be able to save you money on your homeowner's insurance. His company is currently offering a substantial discount for homes with an alarm system and I'd like to review your policy to see what your savings would be."

Bill does the same thing but in reverse. He already knows which clients do not have a security system, so he began contacting his clients to check in and let them know about John who can help them qualify for a discount and offer superior home security at the same time.

They worked it out and this became an incredible source of business for both of them!"

## Conflict Resolution, Member Training and Quality Control

An unfortunate by-product of any organization involving people is conflict among members. As Power Team Leader it is your job to help resolve issues among members and maintain quality control by reviewing and either approving or declining new applications for membership.

How you go about policing your group is up to you. One of the big advantages of joining a structured networking group is the system already in place to manage all aspects of the group, including conflict resolution and ongoing training to keep the Power Team running efficiently and effectively.

### Ivan's Perspective
*"Networking and Friends"*

*"One of the strengths of a good networking group is that most of the members become friends. And ironically, one of the weaknesses is that most of the members become friends. It's both a strength and weakness. Accountability becomes key in running a good network because friends don't like to hold friends accountable. But, people who **get** networking don't have a problem with system and structure.*

*It's easy for a networking group that meets regularly to become a coffee talk session with little or no networking going on. That's exactly what happens when a group loses, or never has to begin with, a purpose, focus, system and structure.*

*People begin to make up their own stuff and the networking loses focus. When you lose focus the meetings become social. Networking should be about business. Of course there has to be a social aspect, but it's really about business, commitment and accountability.*

*People are like water and will take the path of least resistance. Without a framework to operate in, the agenda becomes the topic of the day, whatever the person running the group thinks the meeting should be about. That sort of inconsistency over time is a problem for a networking group.*

*Even if you have a good strong leader, at some point the person's life will change or maybe he or she will simply get burned out. The problem starts if there is no one else to teach. Teaching is a leaky-bucket process. You start with a whole bucket of information. When that information is taught to someone else, some of that information leaks out and the people being taught only get that limited version of the information. In turn, when that person teaches someone else, the material continues to get watered down based on their understanding and ability to articulate the material.*

*By the time you are in the third or fourth generation of people passing along the information, you only have about half a bucket remaining. When the bucket of information gets low, people start putting in their own stuff. Very rarely does the material improve over time with this process."*

*– Dr. Ivan Misner*

# Section II
## Start Bragging!

**Bragging Buddy Tip:** *"Facts Tell But Stories Sell!"*

*Successful Bragging Buddies tell great stories. Why? Telling a terrific story is a powerful way to help prospects like and trust someone they haven't even met, in this case the networking partner you are referring.*

*Familiarize yourself with the success stories on the pages to follow. Pick up ideas, find new connections and then go learn your networking partners success stories. Learn them well enough to comfortably retell and make a favorable impression when giving a testimonial to a targeted prospect. As a result, you will become a more compelling Bragging Buddy and your Power Team's number-one referral source!*

# *Start Bragging!*

Your success with the Money on the Table system is ultimately based on five simple, yet essential skills:

1)  Identify your most productive Key Situations and targeted prospects based on your business category and Contact Sphere

2)  Build a Power Team of networking partners from both inside and outside your own Contact Sphere who also target the same Key Situations and targeted prospects

3)  Systematically make your network visible to increase opportunity for targeted prospects to ask about a Power Team product or service of interest

4)  Consistently recognize the Six Key Situations and your Power Team's targeted prospects (referral opportunities) when they cross your path

5)  Confidently initiate conversation and give compelling Bragging Buddy testimonials to targeted prospects

The rest of this book gives a name and puts a face to money on the table you've been overlooking by failing to employ these five skills. Chapters 13-18 show you how to uncover referral opportunities by systematically making your network visible, as well as how to recognize targeted prospects and create referrals with compelling testimonials from each of the Six Key Situations for 36 popular business categories spanning all six Contact Spheres.

In addition to helpful hints on recognizing targeted prospects across the array of industry groups, we include examples of specific trigger questions you can use to uncover referral opportunities in every conversation you have with a targeted prospect.

**Chapter 13**

# *Business Builder 36+ Referrals*

People "Building a business," "Trying to make money" or "Increase sales" are experiencing the "Business Builder" Key Situation. Business Builders are the primary target market for the Business Services Contact Sphere:

- Business Coaching and Training

- Mobile Telecommunications

- Computer Products and Services

- Office Machines Sales and Service

- Printing and Graphics

- Thank You (Gift Baskets) and Promotional Products

These six Business Services categories are examples of a broader spectrum of products and services aimed at helping people run a business.

While helping their clients and customers, people in these business categories can be trained to find money on the table for your business as well, even if you are not directly or traditionally related to the Business Services Contact Sphere.

Focus on recognizing the Business Builder Key Situation as the first step in the sequence of creating referrals.

### *"Business Builder" Target Market's Basic Needs:*

- Increase Marketing Exposure

- Increase Sales

- Reduce Overhead

- Save Time

- Asset and Operations Management

## Referrals to Other Industries

Business Services categories are in position to create an ongoing stream of referrals to real estate and finance categories for the "business of business" products and services of insurance, accounting, legal advice, financial planning and buying or selling real estate.

Referrals also fly to both the personal and property services categories to take care of day-to-day tasks and free up the Business Builder's time to do more business. On a related theme, wellness categories get referrals to help the Business Builder feel more energized with increased endurance both mentally and physically. Finally, the events categories receive referrals to help stimulate sales by bringing attention to a business through special events and promotions.

Over time, your Bragging Buddy efforts will put money on the table for the entire Power Team. As soon as you are perceived as a Golden Goose of money-making referrals, your Power Team partners will not hesitate to go the extra mile, and, in return, find money on the table for you!

## Trigger Questions

Regardless of your business category, once you identify that someone you meet or already know is a Business Builder, your referral recognition alarm flashes green and you begin asking questions to uncover a need your Power Team can solve.

The following trigger questions are fast and effective tools to start turning money on the table into money-making referrals:

- *There are so many different things going on when you are trying to build a business... what would you say is your biggest challenge right now?*

- *So aside from all this business-building stuff, what's the next big event coming up for you?*

Now you have the prospect talking and you must listen carefully. Do you have a Power Team partner who can be of service? Continue asking questions to uncover a need. Here are Business Builder Key Situation follow up trigger questions and success stories to give you ideas on how to create referrals for 36 popular business categories.

## Business Services

**Computers** Do you have a reliable and knowledgeable computer pro to create your website and help market your business online using blogs and social media?

Do you have a good computer pro to keep your computers virus free and your network running smoothly?

**Business Coaching** Are you taking advantage of a structured business training and personal development system that helps you be the best you can be and achieve peak performance?

---

*Todd Garland* – The Referral Institute: "Don't Reinvent the Wheel"

"On-going training and education gives someone building a business easy and affordable access to expert training, case studies, processes, procedures and strategies that they might not have thought about otherwise. In other words, don't try to reinvent the wheel. Although all business owners believe they have a great idea and are unique, businesses in general are not unique.

What is unique is having an idea—a product or a service—bringing it to market and generating income. Someone who is building a business needs access to an ongoing stream of current, new information, tools and systems from today's top experts in virtually every aspect of building a successful business. Successful people know the value of ongoing training and personal development."

---

**Printing** Would your business benefit from a professional, printed newsletter to your clients and prospects?

Are you using your printed materials to build your brand? My printer can even customize the appearance of standard business contracts with your branding image, logo and message.

Does your business use carbonless "Production Tickets" to track the process of an order, job or account?

Do you have a good, reliable printer for your business cards, letterhead, brochures and signs?

### Beth M. Anderson – BethMAnderson.com: "New Business is Big Business"

*"A person visited our networking group who was just starting a business after many years of working for somebody else. The printer was one of the first people to do business with him for business cards and stationary, in addition to the graphic designer who did the logo. The banker helped him set up a separate business bank account and the accountant got his bookkeeping in order, in terms of knowing what to keep track of for deductions and tax prep.*

*The business coach helped him figure out what to do next and how to move forward. He worked with the lawyer to set up the right business entity, whether it be a Sole Proprietor, an LLC, or Sub Chapter S. The gentleman had never heard of errors and omissions insurance, so of course he worked with the insurance agent in our group. The computer expert worked with him to get a new computer system and also set it up into a network for his new business. It was amazing to see how many people in our group he did business with!"*

**Promotional Products** Do you have a really sharp promotional products person who can match the right item at the right price to reach your target market?

Have you thought about customized calendar magnets, pens, coffee mugs or other promotional products to help your customers and clients remember you?

**Telecommunications** Do you have a good telecommunications person who can help you save money on long-distance phone bills with a Voice Over Internet Phone system?

Are you paying too much for Internet and cell phones?

### Jack Casteneda –Telecom: "Golf Course Communications"

*"We primarily work with businesses and I do a lot of networking, regardless of where I am. One day, I was out on the golf course and struck up a conversation with another golfer. I told him that I was a rep for all the major carriers for phone service with land lines, wireless*

and Internet, sort of like an independent broker for communication providers, and that I really enjoyed going into companies that had large cell phone bills and seeing how we could reduce those bills. I told him my fee was contingent on producing money-saving results.

He was very interested and said, "I just took over the CFO position at my company and the cell phone bills are over $10,000 a month. You've got to help me!"

I didn't change their carrier but I did adjust the products and services they were using. I cut their cell phone bill down about 35%, to $6,500 from $10,000.

That led to working on their land lines. They must have had five or six different carriers. I put him into a plan with everything under one carrier and cut that bill by $1,500 a month down to $3,500.

So that's what I do, I simplify business telecommunications and help people save money."

**Thank You Gifts**  Do you work with a local gift basket maker to "brand" your custom gift baskets to your company image or chocolate truffle company that can put your logo on a box of chocolates to help you say "Thank You" to your clients and customers?

How do you recognize your best clients on occasions like a birthday, new baby, get well or sympathy? An experienced, professional and local gift basket or chocolate truffle company can help.

Do you know what is considered an appropriate "Thank You" for a referral you've received?  I work with a local gift basket company that specializes in referral gifts.

---

*Jenifer Anseth* — M.R. Designs & Gifts: "Tax Relief Gift Baskets for CPAs"

"A financial planner from another BNI Chapter found me through the BNI Website and her goal was to get face time with her existing CPA referral sources, as well as introduce herself to other CPAs, and around tax time that's a near impossible thing to do.

She wanted to take something with her like a "Tax Relief" gift basket. So we put together all sorts of thoughtful things like chicken noodle soup, aspirin, a little poem, stress-relief fist squeezers, fruit snacks, power bars, and energy drinks."

*She would visit local CPAs. When she showed up with the gift, she had no problem getting the CPAs out of their office and in the lobby within minutes to see her.*

*For her it is a way to get face-to-face with her referral sources, just reminding them that she was available to them. She always has new brochures, lets them know how much she appreciates their referrals and reminds them of one or two common situations when she can be of help as a financial planner.*

*A lot of times, the CPAs may know these referral situations are good for the financial planner but when their heads are down and they're busy, they forget. This is her way of getting face time with her CPAs at tax time. She does it every year, so something's working!"*

## *Events Business Categories*

Events business categories can focus primarily on increasing sales through special events and client/customer appreciation. If you ask your Business Builder prospect, "What is your biggest challenge as you build your business?" and the answer is "increasing sales" or "building our brand and name recognition," think about your Power Team partners from the Events Contact Sphere as a possible solution.

**Caterer**  Do you have a caterer who makes great food, gives friendly service and is very reliable for your office open house, product launch, or next special event?

---

### *Mary Ellen Rae – Personal Touch Gourmet: "Extra Special Open House"*

*"I had a client who was joining a financial planning group as a new financial advisor. She hired me for an open house at her new office.*

*My client wanted to bring past clients from before she joined this company and to also invite friends and family to build her business. She was helping her current network, the people she invited to see her beautiful new office and meet the professional team of people there so they could then give great testimonials when talking to other people and creating referrals for her.*

*It was very important to her for people to see the beautiful suite of offices she would now be working in. It really was a great office in an upscale community which helps people associate that success to her in her new business venture."*

**Event Planner**  Have you thought of working with an experienced event planner for a very special launch event to promote your new product or service?

Do you have an experienced event planner for a grand opening to jump start your business?

Have you thought of working with an experienced event planner for a client appreciation party or extra special holiday party to increase the referrals you receive from satisfied customers and vendors?

**Florist**  Do you have a florist you can trust to bring fresh flowers once a week and make sure all the plants in your store or office stay healthy and look great?

**Jeweler**  Are you working with an experienced jeweler to create a special gift to reward your most valuable employee?

Have you considered "Cash for Gold" with a trusted local jeweler to generate some cash flow from old jewelry to build your business?

**Limousine Service**  Have you made arrangements with a reputable limo service to take high profile clients to the airport or corporate events, as well as to reward your top employee with a special night on the town?

---

*Joe Greco – Limousine Service: "Experience and Reliability"*

*"I work with some huge companies, Price Waterhouse Cooper, and NASDAQ, for example, who hire me when they have people coming and going to my area in upstate New York. My motto is "Experience and Reliability." My business customers put a premium on being on time and we make sure that we are never late, that the cars are clean and that our drivers are courteous and professional. We require our drivers to have a dual license, not only with the Motor Vehicles Bureau but also the Limousine Commission. We have a safety protocol that we follow every morning to make sure in advance that we will be ready for our appointments during the day. That's the attention to detail that keeps our business clients coming back."*

**Photographer**  Are you working with an experienced, professional photographer for headshots or product and location images to use on business cards, promotional materials and your website?

# Personal Services Business Categories

Personal Services business categories serve the Business Builder's need to save time, increase convenience and improve their quality of life.

**Auto Repair**  Do you have a good auto mechanic you can trust to keep your company vehicles safe and reliable?

Did you know you can save money with regularly scheduled vehicle maintenance to avoid costly repairs?

---

### Bill Coniam – 25th Street Automotive: "Auto Financial Planner"

*"I like to view the job of an auto mechanic as being a kind of a financial planner—your automotive financial planner. Assess your current situation, look at your goals and make a financial plan for down the road to make it happen."*

**Errands/Delivery**  Do you have someone you can count on to pick up/deliver and run errands while you are busy building the business?

Are you concerned about the cost and liability of your employees driving around for errands, mail and supplies pick up or product deliveries?

**Greeting Cards**  Do you have an easy to use, computer-based follow-up system to mail actual, top-quality greeting cards in your own handwriting, with the option of including photos for clients, prospects, referral sources and vendors?

---

### Nathan Dominguez – BNI Arizona and Send Out Cards: "Four-Way Follow Up"

*"I have a business broker in my networking group who, every time he speaks to someone about a merger or an acquisition, he immediately refers them to me and greeting cards as an easy and very effective marketing and introduction campaign. The major benefit to these businesses is getting instant exposure and visibility with their own database in four different ways: We train people to follow up with prospects, customers, referral sources and vendors, and the results are amazing!"*

**Pet Services**  Do you have someone you can trust for dog walks and empty house visits while you are busy building your business?

*Kevin McClure* – *Leashes and Leads, Pet Services :*
*"More Dog Walks and More Time for Business"*

*"We have a general contractor client who is new in town. With the amount of travel and time he's put into building his business, he began to feel he was neglecting his pets. This happens often, whether it's through building a business or people in everyday work situations.*

*We can either come out to their home to walk and feed their dog, or they can bring their pet to us where the pets can come and get a balanced mixture of supervised rest and play sessions. In addition to the sheer convenience of having us work with the pets, the owner also gets the added benefit at the end of a day that their dog is relatively calm because it has had an active day rather than being locked up at home. Our clients love this."*

**Personal Chef**  Do you have a personal chef to make sure you eat healthy, home-cooked meals (at a surprisingly affordable price) so you can stay busy building your business?

**Travel Agent**  Have you thought of working with a professional travel agent to take care of the details for your next corporate event or to create a special "Dream Vacation" promotion for your business?

*Bernice L. Strauber* – *Travel Agent: "Value-Added Service"*

*"I work with a lot of meeting planners from corporations or owners of small businesses. What I do can be as simple as suggesting some places with the facilities and types of equipment they might need for their meeting to booking flights and hotel reservations."*

## *Property Services Business Categories*

Like Personal Services, business categories in Property Services help the Business Builder save time or money.

**Cleaning**  Do you have someone you can trust to keep your office clean and also clean your home while you are building your business?

Hiring a professional carpet cleaner can save you a lot of time, it's not as expensive as you might think, and it will make your office cleaner and more professional looking.

**Furniture Sales** Do you know someone who can find new and used office furniture at a great price?

**General Contractor** Do you need a licensed contractor who can build from the ground up or do remodel and repair work on your retail store or office building?

---

### Hazel Walker – BNI and Referral Institute: "Built From BNI"

"Dr. Jeremy Ciano, an ophthalmologist who is a BNI member in one of my chapters, decided to leave a national chain to open his own optometry store. He will tell you that his entire business has been built from BNI.

It all started with a BNI general contractor who built his new store. That led to the painting contractor, then the insurance agent wrote health and life insurance policies for the employees. He was referred to the CPA and the attorney for all the contracts and legal issues. He was a referral to the payroll service for all his payroll needs. It just kept rolling for him. Every piece of his business was built by referral."

---

**Interior Design** Do you have a talented and resourceful interior designer to make your office more appealing to your customers and clients, as well as operate more efficiently?

**Landscaping** Do you have a reliable landscaper to take care of your home's exterior so you have more time to build your business?

**Security Systems** Do you have a security system to protect your office or cameras for theft prevention and keeping an eye on things when you are not there? Do you need a way to make sure only trusted employees can get into certain areas of your building?

## Real Estate/Finance Business Categories

Real Estate/Finance business categories primarily serve the Business Builder's need for various aspects of asset and operations management.

**Attorney (Business)** Do you have a good attorney to review your business contracts, as well as create a Will or a Trust to protect your assets?

## Robert Gross – Attorney: "Vending Machines are a Business"

"People starting a new business need to meet with an attorney, but unfortunately, in many cases they don't realize this. I had a client in my networking group as a dance instructor who left the group to open a vending machine business. I told him that even though it seemed like the type of business you could do informally, he needed to form a company to protect himself.

You need to run things as a business. Other businesses are not going to deal with you as an individual, you need to look professional and form a company. I'm not a tax attorney, but you are going to want the tax benefits of running a company. There are also liability issues and you need to protect yourself.

Working with the CPA in my networking group who advised him on the best and most cost effective entity for taxes, I set up an LLC (Limited Liability Company) to insulate my client personally from liability in the event there was a lawsuit against his company.

Now he is able to sign contracts with both suppliers for the vending machine snacks, as well as the building owners where he places his machines. So now when he walks into a building to talk to the owner, or these large real estate and commercial management companies, he's not some guy in a pickup truck coming in with a bunch of snacks, he has a company name, a truck with a corporate logo on it, and is much more professional when he hands them a contract to sign. The clients appreciate the fact that he looks official and he's done well because of it.

**CPA** Do you have a CPA to save money on tax planning and preparation?

**Financial Planner** Do you have someone to help you make smart investments for your retirement as well as your employees?

## John Chichester – Financial Planning: "Wealth and Wellness"

"Back in 2003, I met with a doctor client of mine. He is a spine and sports doctor, a specialist called a Physiatrist. He had five employees and wanted to put in a retirement plan. At the time, his current plan maxed out at about a $30,000 annual contribution for himself.

Six years later, he has grown to over 30 employees and he has three other doctors working for him. Not only do we still have the 401K Profit Share Plan, but we also have a Cash Benefit Plan.

*This owner is now putting in about $100,000 a year for himself. His wife, who is a nurse and also on staff, is putting in about $50,000 for herself. So they went from $30,000 to about $150,000 in six years. He also puts away a lot for all his employees and two other doctors who are maximizing what they are putting away as well.*

*This client now has about $350,000 in his account and about $150,000 in his wife's account. So over the past six years, he's been able to put away about $500,000 that he did not have before working with me. And he saved on the taxes on all the money he put in.*

*His employees' accounts are very high, as well. They look at it as money they would not have if they weren't working with this individual. His employees know that he is very generous and as a result they stay. Most of them have been there for the full six years that I've been working with him. His business continues to grow, he has very little turnover and he feels like he is doing the right thing for his employees and for himself."*

**Insurance**  Do you have an insurance agent to protect your business with errors and omissions insurance, as well as to provide your family and employees with life, health and disability insurance?

**Mortgages**  Do you have a mortgage officer who can help you take some equity out of your house to pay for special projects or equipment to build your business?

**Realtor**  Do you have an experienced Realtor who can help you invest in your own office building, retail location or manufacturing facility rather than lease space and build equity for someone else? Do you have a Realtor you can trust to find a larger house with a perfect home office space you can use to build your business?

---

### Kristie Smith  *– Realtor: "Home Office Business Builder"*

*"I have a client in the financial industry who had a corporate job with a huge company and was offered a buy-out as part of a downsizing move. He took it and decided to go in a completely different direction.*

*For the family it was great to have Dad home, but it was not working out for him. The space wasn't right, there was too much noise in the area of the house near the room he could use as an office, and the family just wasn't used to boundaries and never knowing if the dad was working or not.*

*They decided to purchase a new home that had a nice finished basement including an office area for the dad. It's working out great! The kids don't go down into the basement during the day when the dad is working. So now for family dynamics and efficiency at home, he gets to work at home in a separate area and it's a lot easier for the rest of the family as well."*

## Wellness Business Categories

Wellness business categories serve a crossover need, helping the Business Builder save both time and money with improved energy and better overall health.

**Chiropractor** Do you have a chiropractor to help ease your aches and pains so you can be at your best while building your business?

**Life Coach** Are you working with an experienced life coach to help you set and achieve your goals and stay on track with your business plan?

---

*Judith Joyce – Journey Beyond Belief : Life Coach: "Business Values"*

*"I've helped a number of clients who started a new business. A big piece revolves around the values they have for their life, which many times carries forward into their business. That seems to be a new concept for a lot of people who are starting a new business: thinking about what is really important to them. Things like honesty, integrity, the environment and sustainability.*

*Being in touch with their values will affect their marketing, branding, customer service, as well as the actual products or services they affiliate themselves with. I help people make sure the heart of their business doesn't get lost in the financial side of what they are doing. Sometimes that also includes making sure the website and any social networking online reflects the person's core values as well."*

**Massage** Have you thought of working with a massage therapist to reward employees (and yourself), increase office efficiency and improve morale?

### Lisa D. Rossi, LMT – Massage Therapy:
"Hairstylists, Foot Rubs, and Making More Money"

"I have a massage space in a salon. After the stylists hear how much better my clients feel as they are leaving the salon, a few have started coming to me as well because they feel it makes a difference in what they are doing, since in their professions they are on their feet all the time. It helps them make more money because they feel better, they have more energy and their clients pick up on that. They wind up getting more referrals because the whole experience at the salon is more fun and they tell their friends about it."

### Alina Pellicer, LMT – Massage Therapy:
"Better Golf, Better Breathing, Better Referrals"

"I have several clients who are friends who golf together. One of them really felt great results from massage work, with reduced back pain and fewer aches and pains in general. Not only did he notice the improvement, but so did his golfing buddies. A few started to become regular clients and they tell lots of other people about me.

One of them is in sales and covers a territory that includes San Diego, Phoenix, Tucson and Las Vegas, so he does a lot of driving. He told me that he's now using in his business a breathing exercise I showed him to relieve his stress on the golf course. He says the combination of massage and all the other tips and techniques I help him with allows him to do his work more efficiently and reduces a lot of the stress from all the driving time going from one client to the next."

**Nutrition**  Are you taking nutritional products to help you maintain optimal brain function and increase stamina while building your business?

**Personal Trainer**  Do you know a personal trainer to help you keep your energy level up and stay in great shape while building your business?

### Taru Fisher – Personal Fitness: "More Stamina, More Energy, More Business"

"We have a woman in our networking group with a physical challenge who uses a cane. She is a kitchen and bath designer and has to go to a lot of different places and look at peoples' homes. She started working with us and now rarely needs to use the cane. We do strength training. Slow motion, high intensity, low impact, "safe strength" training once or twice a week for 20 minutes. She gets 50% stronger than if she went to *a traditional gym every day. She's a lot more mobile, has more stamina and energy when she's inside a client's home. It's made her job easier, she can work longer if she wants to and she enjoys it more."*

**Water Treatment** Do you know a water quality professional to make sure you, your employees and customers are drinking healthy water? Are you paying too much for bottled water at the workplace?

---

*Brian McCowin* – McCowin Enterprises, Water Treatment: "Liquid Assets"

*"I was referred to a client who had a factory that makes mirrors. He was paying between $500 and $600 for bottled water for his many employees to drink. We put in a few "Bottleless" coolers that hook up to a water source, filter the water and make pure water on the spot rather than bringing it in with bottles. Now he pays $90 a month. It's a lot less, the dollar amount doesn't vary and it takes care of all his employees. There's also the added convenience of not having to store the bottles, as well as removing the liability and Workman's Compensation issues of an employee hurting themselves while lifting a bottle or exposing people to bacteria if they don't clean the bottle top before turning it upside down into the water cooler."*

**Chapter 14**

# *Getting Healthy 36+ Referrals*

People in the "Getting Healthy" Key Situation are recovering from illness or injury, getting in shape or losing weight. These people are the primary target market for the Wellness Contact Sphere:

- Chiropractor
- Life Coach
- Massage
- Nutrition
- Personal Trainer
- Water/Air Quality

These six Wellness Contact Sphere business categories are examples of a broader spectrum of products and services aimed at health and wellness.

While helping their clients and customers, people in these business categories can be trained to find money on the table for your business as well, even if you are not directly or traditionally related to the health and wellness industry.

Focus on recognizing the Getting Healthy Key Situation as the first step in the sequence of creating referrals.

## *"Getting Healthy" Target Market's Basic Needs*

- Help recovering from illness or injury
- Help with responsibilities they cannot do for themselves
- Support in losing weight or to stop smoking
- Training and coaching in proactive wellness

## Referrals to Other Industries

People in Wellness Contact Sphere business categories are in a position to find an ongoing stream of qualified referrals for both the Personal and Property Services Contact Spheres. Business categories in both groups provide value by performing day-to-day tasks the person getting healthy cannot or should not be doing on his own.

Not so easy or direct are business categories from Real Estate/Finance, Business Services and most of all, the Events Contact Sphere. Although more random and less frequent, people getting healthy do need the products and services of these industry groups from time to time in their daily life.

*Over time, your systematic Bragging Buddy efforts will put money on the table for the entire Power Team.* As soon as you are perceived as a Golden Goose of money-making referrals, your Power Team partners will not hesitate to go the extra mile, and in return find money on the table for you!

## Trigger Questions

Regardless of your business category, once you realize that someone you meet or already know is in a Getting Healthy Key Situation, you can begin asking questions to uncover a need your Power Team can solve.

The following trigger questions are fast and effective tools to start turning money on the table into money-making referrals:

- *I am glad to know that you are on the road to recovery. Congratulations! Are there any challenges at home or otherwise that you could use some help with?*

- *While getting healthy, what's the next big event coming up for you?*

Now that you have the prospect talking, you must listen carefully. Do you have a Power Team partner who can be of service? Continue asking questions to uncover a need. Here are Getting Healthy Key Situation follow up trigger questions and success stories to give you ideas on how to create referrals for 36 popular business categories.

# Business Services

Business Service categories sometimes require a bit of imagination to find money on the table in the Getting Healthy Key Situation. In many cases, the referral opportunity is to a nonprofit or other organization that works in support of a cure for the illness or therapy for the injury involved.

**Cell phones** Do you and your spouse have a new safety device that reduces the microwaves coming out of your cell phone?

**Computers** Do you have a computer pro to keep your computers working, to remove any computer viruses, or install new equipment? Are you involved with any type of nonprofit health and wellness organization that could use a computer pro?

**Business Coaching** Are you using a business coach to help with the work/life balance and personal development required to stop smoking or to set and achieve fitness and weight loss goals that last a lifetime, rather than a short while?

**Printing** Do you have a reliable printer for the nonprofit organization or community group you are involved in?

**Promotional Products** Are you involved with a health and wellness nonprofit organization that can use customized magnets and other promotional items for fund-raising events and activities?

---

*Patrick Finley* – Art Promotional Services, LLC: "Heavy Promotion"

*"When a friend, Steven, was trying to lose 300 pounds, he wanted to do some magnets to promote his blog—a journal of his weight-loss program. A good friend of ours told Steven that if he lost the 300 pounds he would send him on an all-expense-paid VIP trip to the races at Talladega. So we created some magnets with the word "Talledega" and logo plus a car on there, and that's how he's promoting his blog (www.whoatemyblog.com) and getting people to follow him and, in the process, give him moral support."*

# Events Business Categories

The Events business categories are not an easy match for the Getting Healthy Key Situation. But people in all stages of health and wellness have other events in their life that can lead to referrals for the Events business categories. In addition, you can create referrals by shifting the focus beyond the person you are talking with, to events for a nonprofit or other organization that works with their particular illness or injury.

**Caterer** Does the nonprofit organization that works with your particular illness or injury have a great caterer for their fundraisers and other functions?

**Event Planner** Does the nonprofit organization that works with your particular illness or injury have an event planner for their fundraisers and other functions?

**Florist** Do you have a florist who brings in fresh flowers to keep your surroundings in the recovery room bright and cheerful?

---

### Sheri Cervantes – Florist : "Flowers Show You Care"

*"When someone is recovering from illness or injury, receiving flowers makes him or her feel special, that he or she is not alone, that people really do care."*

**Jeweler** Are you working with an experienced jeweler to create a beautiful charm bracelet to celebrate your return to wellness or as a reward for reaching a goal, like stop smoking or lose weight?

---

### Morris Esses – Jeweler: "Cigarette Reward"

*"Over the past ten years, the woman self purchaser has become the most important buyer in our jewelry business. Years ago, men would come into the store and buy a gift for their loved one, their spouse, their children. Today it's a situation where the women are earning their own money and they are buying gifts for themselves. Many are rewarding themselves for different things they've accomplished with a special gift. As an example, if someone has lost 20 or 30 pounds and is feeling great about herself, she might come in and treat herself to a gift.*

*Two women came into the store one day and told us that one had $2,100 to spend, the other had $1,000, and they wanted to buy themselves gifts. They had both stopped smoking about a year earlier and every day they would set aside the money they had been spending on cigarettes, which for one of them was six dollars a day. (She was the one with $2,100.)*

*She bought herself a beautiful bracelet. She came back many times for different repairs and watch batteries and smaller gifts during the year. Guess what? The following year she came back in the store and had $2,100 to spend again. This has happened three years running!"*

**Limousine Service** Have you made arrangements with a limo service for the trips to the doctor or the hospital?

**Photographer** Are you working with an experienced, professional photographer for a "See how GREAT I look!" recovery or weight-loss photo?

---

*Tani Dugger – Insight Photography:*
*"Breast Cancer Awareness Calendar Photos"*

*"One of the breast cancer awareness groups in the area approached us with an idea for a calendar for survivors of the disease. So we had all the people they had chosen for the calendar come into the studio and took pictures of them showing their scars. We were very happy to be the photographers who helped with that."*

## Personal Services Business Categories

**Auto Repair** Do you want to make sure your vehicle is still safe to drive after an accident? Do you have an auto mechanic you can trust to keep your family vehicles safe and reliable? Did you know you can save money with regularly scheduled vehicle maintenance to avoid costly repairs?

---

*Bill Coniam – 25th Street Automotive: "Vehicle Safety"*

*"People who have been in a car accident understand the importance of vehicle safety. We get a good number of people who say, "I was in an accident and while the insurance is going to take out the dents and paint my car, I don't feel comfortable." So we inspect the vehicle from a mechanical and safety angle as opposed to the cosmetics that are normally addressed at a body shop."*

**Errands/Delivery** Do you have someone to pick up groceries and run errands while you are on the road to wellness? Does your home health care provider need help with medical or dental related deliveries to your home?

**Greeting Cards** Would you like to send top-quality greeting cards from the comfort of your own home computer while you are recovering?

Do you have an easy-to-use, computer-based system to mail top-quality greeting cards in your own handwriting, with the option of including photos to connect with friends and family and to say "Thank You" for helping with your recovery?

---

*Nathan Dominguez – BNI Arizona and Send Out Cards:*
*"Thank You Cards from Home"*

*"Thanks to technology, now people who are laid up at home have the ability to send great quality cards, delivered in the mail, from their computer. It's a really easy way to thank people who have helped in someone's recovery or reconnect to loved ones with a lot more impact than email."*

**Pet Services** Do you have someone you can trust for dog walks and empty house visits while your health improves?

---

*Kevin McClure – Leashes and Leads, Pet Services: "Serenity Park"*

*"A common situation here in Rochester, with the Mayo Clinic, is the patient who stays in town four to eight weeks for treatment. Many times they don't want to leave their dogs at home, and sometimes it's not possible.*

*We have quite a few patients who bring their animals, which has become a target market for us. As part of our boarding services, we've integrated an area here on our property and call it "Serenity Park." The idea is to have walking paths with beautiful landscaping, bushes, trees and flowers to allow those patients to come at any time of the day and go on a beautiful walk with their dog. Just being around animals in general is good for the health."*

**Personal Chef** Do you have a personal chef to make sure you eat healthy, home-cooked meals while on the road to wellness?

---

*Mary Ellen Rae – Personal Touch Gourmet : "Drop-Off Dinners"*

*"I do "Drop-Off Dinners," which are very popular for families or friends of someone who is going through a very difficult time. In one instance, I was contacted by a friend of a referral partner who wanted to help a family out where the mom was going through chemotherapy for cancer. I dropped off fresh, hot and ready-to-eat dinners each night. All they had to do was sit down and eat.*

*I've used Drop-Off Dinners for a lot of families. It's a great way for stressed-out and maybe physically-unable families to feed their family with nutritious, fresh and tasty food.*

*Another service I offer is cooking classes for groups or individuals. I use lots of healthy ingredients.*

*One client came to me after making a decision to change her unhealthy diet. I did a private cooking class for her. I went to her house and went through her kitchen, looked through the pantry to see what she had in her cabinets. Of course, we took out all the unhealthy items, things with hidden salts, hidden fats, and whatever else that needed to go.*

*We cleaned out the cabinets and talked about how important it is to get off the processed foods and plan her meals in advance, which really comes into play during grocery shopping. Having a shopping list really helped her avoid the pitfalls of going food shopping when she was starving and buying all the really bad stuff.*

*I also helped her find a personal trainer, so this woman was successful in losing weight because she was able change the types of foods she was eating, along with becoming more active with professionally supervised exercise."*

**Travel Agent**   Have you taken advantage of the experience and discount pricing of a professional travel agent who can save you money creating a great vacation to look forward to as your health returns?

### Bernice L. Strauber – *Travel Agent: "Power of Firsthand Experience"*

*"I am a big fan of the therapeutic baths in Europe. I have one client who goes regularly to one outside of Prague in the Czech Republic. It's a wellness clinic.*

*I have been to many places outside of this country, including one in particular in Budapest, where I send a lot of people because of the healing baths there. When I've personally been to these places, I can talk from firsthand experience with my clients and that's something that pays off over and over and they really appreciate it."*

# Property Services Business Categories

**Cleaning** Did you know that professional carpet cleaning can help improve indoor air quality by removing up to 95% of the dirt and allergens in the carpet?

Do you have someone you can trust to clean the kitchen, bathrooms and rest of your house while regaining your health?

Do you have someone you can trust to clean the air-conditioning ducts and use the best filters to make sure you and your family are breathing clean, healthy air inside your home?

**Furniture Sales** Do you know someone who can find the right pieces of furniture that will help you recover faster or sleep better?

**General Contractor** Do you have an experienced, licensed contractor you can trust to remodel or repair your home as you recover from illness or injury?

---

*Joel Zanoff* – *General Contractor: "Zero-Clearance Bathroom"*

*"I had a very good customer who unfortunately had a stroke. She was no longer able to use the bathroom we had remodeled for her about four or five years earlier. In the hospital, I met with her, with her doctors and the rehab people to discuss what we had to do. We created a zero-clearance bathroom, where there's no curb on the shower, grab handles around the commode, basically making it so that when she was in a wheelchair she could just roll into the bathroom and use everything by herself."*

**Interior Design** Do you have an interior designer to create a healing and nurturing environment, as well as help make sure your home is safe and functional while you regain your health?

**Landscaping** Do you have a landscaper to make sure your plants, shrubs, trees and lawn remain in good condition as your regain your health?

**Security Systems** Do you have a medical emergency wrist pendant alarm?

Do you have a good intercom system for the sick room?

Are you testing your air for carbon monoxide?

# Real Estate/Finance Business Categories

**Attorney (Business)** Do you have a good attorney to create a Will or a Trust to protect your family if you were to die?

**Attorney (Personal Injury)** Do you have a good attorney to take care of your medical bills and a lawsuit to get a settlement for your injury?

---

### Robert Gross – Attorney: "Injured in a Nightclub"

*"The CPA in my networking group referred her daughter, who had been injured in a nightclub. I had talked to the group about bars and nightclubs specifically, and the rules and regulations regarding safety there. It really helps to be specific when asking for referrals. Much better than simply saying, "If you know of anyone who has been injured, please have them give me a call," which is too general and doesn't mean anything."*

---

**CPA** Do you have a CPA you can trust to save money on tax planning and preparation?

**Financial Planner** Do you have someone you can trust to help you make smart investments so you will be able to reach your financial goals?

**Insurance** Do you have a good insurance agent to protect you and your family with life, health and disability insurance?

---

### Mike McKee – Andrews & McKee Insurance: "Get Insurance Before You Need It"

*"I have a client who, even though she really couldn't afford the coverage, felt strongly about life insurance, so she took out a policy on herself and also her daughter. That was about seven years ago. Well, three months ago she was diagnosed with cancer.*

*At this point, it gives her a lot of comfort to know that her daughter, who is now 24, will have some money for things like a down payment on a house and not have to struggle so much when her mom is gone. The thing is getting people to take out the coverage before they need it, like this woman did."*

---

**Mortgages** Do you have a knowledgeable mortgage officer who can help you take some equity out of your house to pay for any extra bills you may have while you regain your health?

**Realtor** Do you have an experienced Realtor who can help you sell your home or purchase a larger home with space for live-in help or a smaller home with less maintenance as you regain your health?

---

*Kristie Smith* – Realtor: "The Real Emotions of Real Estate"

*"We had a client who passed away after a long illness. We are now working with the executor of the estate to sell the property. It can be a very tricky situation because the adult children are also involved and they can have different interests and different personalities.*

*It's an opportunity for us, though, because we are not just selling a home, but a place where three of the adult children grew up. It's an emotional time for everyone. This is not just a real estate transaction, but really it's an opportunity for us to help provide closure for this family."*

# *Wellness Business Categories*

**Chiropractor** Do you have a good chiropractor to help ease your aches and pains while you build your health?

**Life Coach** Are you working with an experienced life coach to help you set goals and maintain your wellness program?

---

*Judith Joyce* – Journey Beyond Belief – Life Coach:
"The Mind-Body Connection"

*"There are a lot of beliefs and emotional issues around illness and recovery. I work a lot with the body/mind/spirit connection so people can really start to see how the things going on in their body connect to their emotional and mental health and how to break through some of their current beliefs to bring all those elements into alignment for their overall well-being so they can start feeling better about themselves."*

**Massage** Do you have a massage therapist who can help you on your road to wellness?

**Nutrition** Are you taking the best nutritional products to help you lose weight, feel great and maintain optimal health?

**Personal Trainer** Do you know a personal trainer to help you lose weight and get in great shape?

**Water Treatment** Do you know a water quality professional to make sure you and your family are drinking, cooking and also showering in clean, healthy water?

---

### Brian McCowin – McCowin Enterprises: "Don't Be Your Own Water Filter!"

"I had a customer suffering from cancer who had just finished chemotherapy. He was told to keep his toxicity level down and so pure water was very important to him. He had to drink a lot of it and he didn't have the strength to carry big bottles of water to use in his home. We put a system in his home with reverse osmosis to give him exactly what he needed in a way that was very convenient for him. That one fell right into our tagline which is, "If you don't filter your water, your body is the filter!"

About five years ago, I mentioned to my networking group that I was looking for anybody with skin problems, because a lot of that comes from the water in this area, and I can fix it. One of the ladies in the group overheard her hairdresser talking about a client who was having hair and skin problems, and my networking partner developed the referral and put me in touch with that person.

I went out to the home, tested the water and found their chlorine levels were about the equivalent of a public swimming pool. We took care of it, and a similar problem with a friend of hers. These were very large, nice homes in the $7 to $15 million dollar range and we put in systems to clean up the water for showering, bathing and drinking water.

Those two women then referred me to a property manager they both know for a really huge, high-end home. He was trying to get a new water treatment system for this estate-size property but wasn't happy with the companies he had talked to, so he called us out to the house and because we were referred by people he knew and trusted, he was open to meeting us. He liked what we offered and what we had to say and hired us to do the water system. This was a great job for us. It was a huge home and it is currently for sale at $75 million."

# Chapter 15

# *Getting Married 36+ Referrals*

**P**eople who are planning a wedding are the primary target market for the Events Contact Sphere:

- Caterer
- Event Planner
- Florist
- Jeweler
- Limousine Service
- Photographer

These six Events Contact Sphere business categories are examples of a broader spectrum of products and services aimed at people getting married.

While serving their clients and customers, people in these business categories can be trained to find money on the table for your business as well, even if you are not directly or traditionally related to the Events Contact Sphere.

Focus on recognizing the Getting Married Key Situation as the first step in the sequence of creating referrals.

## *"Getting Married" Target Market's Basic Needs*

- Details for the wedding ceremony, reception and honeymoon
- Combining two households
- Investing and insuring for the future

## Referrals to Other Industries

Events business categories are in position to find an ongoing stream of qualified referrals for the entire Power Team. Real Estate and Finance are an easy referral for couples planning for the future, securing their investments or buying and selling real estate.

Wellness, Personal and Property Services Contact Spheres also offer a wide variety of products and services that are frequently of value to people getting married.

---

### Beth M. Anderson – BethMAnderson.com: "A Dozen Wedding Referrals"

*"The massage therapist in my networking group is getting married. She did business with the printer for invitations, the Realtor who helped sell both homes and helped the couple buy a new one. The photographer not only did the wedding photos, but also the engagement photos as well.*

*We have a local farmer in our group who also has weddings on her beautiful property, and she worked with them for the ceremony and reception. With their lives changing, the couple also needed new Wills, which was business for the attorney. The travel agent got brought into it for the honeymoon. She literally walked into the meeting one day with referrals for at least twelve people in our group!"*

**Over time, your Bragging Buddy efforts will put money on the table for the entire Power Team.** As soon as you are perceived as a Golden Goose of money-making referrals, your Power Team partners will not hesitate to go the extra mile, and in return find money on the table for you!


## Trigger Questions

Regardless of your business category, once you identify that someone you meet or already know is getting married you begin asking questions to uncover a need your Power Team can solve.

The following trigger questions are fast and effective tools to start turning money on the table into money-making referrals:

- *So, how is everything going with the wedding plans? What's the biggest challenge right now?*

- *So, while you are taking care of all this wedding stuff, what else is going on?*

Now that the prospect is talking you must listen carefully. Do you have a Power Team partner who can be of service? Continue asking questions to uncover a need. Here are Getting Married Key Situation follow-up trigger questions and success stories to help create ideas for referrals to 36 popular business categories.

# Business Services

Business Services may not specifically tie into the wedding itself, but people getting married, like everyone else, may have a need for a product or service from these business categories and by **systematically making your Power Team visible**, you will create referrals that would have otherwise been missed.

**Telecommunications**  Have you checked into saving money on your cell phone bill by combining your separate plans into a Family Minute Plan for both of you?

**Computers**  Are you creating a wedding website with live streaming of the ceremony, videos and downloadable, printable pictures for friends and family who can't be there in person? Will you and your new spouse need any help networking or backing up your home computers?

**Online Education**  Do you and your spouse use an online education system for personal development, family relations and communication skills, to help keep a happy home?

**Printing**  Are you interested in high-end, customized wedding invitations and "Save the Date" cards?

**Promotional Products**  Have you sent out "Save the Date" engagement magnets for your wedding guests to post on their refrigerator?

Have you thought about special engraved pens and wine glasses for the wedding party? Or other unique and special gifts?

**Thank You Gift**  Have you considered using a local company to create custom gift baskets for your family and wedding party? You can even include your weekend's itinerary!

# Events Business Categories

Weddings are the money-on-the-table mother lode for the Events Contact Sphere.

**Caterer** Have you found a caterer who makes great food, gives friendly service and is very reliable for the reception?

---

### Ralph Swagler – Catering: "Cater to the Bride"

*"Whenever we work at a wedding, we usually have the parents or the in-laws come in first, who narrow down the details – the menu, floral arrangements, DJ, etc., then the bride comes in to make final decisions. Then you're back working with the in-laws or the parents again.*

*Your primary customer is the bride, but she's busy with her dresses and bridesmaids, so we make it a point to not bother the bride. It's our job to take problems and details off the bride, not to add more."*

**Event Planner** Are you getting stressed trying to plan everything yourself? Or do you have a professional event planner to make sure everything goes right so you can enjoy your wedding and reception?

**Florist** Do you have a florist you can trust to make everything beautiful at your wedding?

---

### Sheri Cervantes – Florist : "Orange County Bride"

*"I had a bride in her forties who was born and raised in Southern California and was getting married for the first time. She really wanted to incorporate the theme of Orange County. So I came up with the idea to put sliced oranges inside the clear glass vases as the centerpieces. In her bridal bouquet we also put some flowers from succulent plants that you find in this area. She loved the idea and it really expressed something that she felt strongly about."*

**Jeweler** Are you working with an experienced jeweler to create beautiful wedding rings that will last a lifetime?

**Limousine Service** Have you made arrangements with a limo service for the bridal party and special guests?

**Photographer** Are you working with an experienced, professional wedding photographer to capture the lifelong memories of your special day?

*Tani Dugger* – *Insight Photography: "More Than Just Wedding Photos"*

*"I do more than just a wedding day package. I try to get the grooms more involved. If I can get there on the day of the proposal it gets the men really involved. I do the dress selection, so I will go with the bride and her bridesmaids to the bridal shops when they are picking out their dresses. What I'm doing is building a rapport with the bride and her bridesmaids.*

*I also do the wedding rehearsal, which is always fun because it's the first time they are up there together on the altar or at the ceremony site and you can see the nervousness in them, and I like to capture that as well.*

*So, by the day of the wedding, I am pretty good friends with the couple and we have a lot of fun taking the pictures."*

## Personal Services Business Categories

New responsibilities and time management challenges for people getting married put a regular supply of money on the table for the Personal Services business categories.

**Auto Repair** Do you have a good auto mechanic you can trust to keep your family vehicles safe and reliable? Did you know you can save money with regularly scheduled vehicle maintenance to avoid costly repairs?

**Errands/Delivery** Do you have someone you can count on to pick up groceries and run errands while you are busy with the wedding? Do you need any last minute help running around or picking up things for the wedding?

**Greeting Cards** Do you have an easy-to-use, computer-based system to mail top-quality greeting cards in your own handwriting, with the option of including photos as well, for wedding invitations and thank-you cards?

*Nathan Dominguez* – *BNI Arizona and Send Out Cards:*
*"Wedding Thank You Card Blues"*

*"A lot of brides dread the fact that after the wedding is over, they've got tons of handwriting to do with thank-you cards. And the kicker is that they almost always have a common theme to the cards, where the first one or two lines were basically the same, "Dear Bob, thanks for coming to the wedding! We really enjoyed seeing you."*

*Even though the cards are almost all cookie cutter, they are hand-written and personalized at the bottom, "Thank you for the blender, we look forward to making lots of smoothies!" Our cards do all this on the computer, including the handwriting and signature in a fast, fun way.*

*The event planner in my networking group is now recommending our greeting card service to help brides save lots of time and actually look forward to sending out customized thank-you cards in the mail, with photos, and personalized massages, but in a fraction of the time and cost.*

*The cards also work great to send a card with a photo from the honeymoon and then anniversaries, babies, Christmas and New Year's, you name it. Friends and family usually keep all the cards with the photos because they make a tremendous impact."*

**Pet Services** Do you have someone you can trust for dog walks and empty house visits while you are out of town for your honeymoon?

---

### Kevin McClure *– Leashes and Leads, Pet Services: "Honeymoon Petcam"*

*"One of the features we have for couples on a honeymoon, or on a vacation of any type, are free web cameras we have integrated in our facility. People can literally go anywhere in the world, log onto our website and see their dogs. It puts them at ease so they can relax and enjoy their honeymoon or vacation.*

*Once the honeymoon is over, a lot of couples who are moving in together for the first time take advantage of our training facility. We have a variety of classes that help the two dogs get along with each other, as well as accepting the other spouse as a new owner. We create an opportunity for the owners and the pets to bond and be trained with the new family dynamic."*

**Personal Chef** Do you have a personal chef to make sure you and your spouse eat healthy, home-cooked meals when you both go back to work?

**Travel Agent** Have you taken advantage of the experience and discount pricing of a professional travel agent who can save you money and make sure you have a great honeymoon?

### *Bernice L. Strauber* – *Travel Agent: "Honeymoon Travel"*

*"I helped book a great honeymoon for a couple—Tahiti, Bora-Bora and Maori. Since then they've referred me to many other clients who may or may not have been getting married, but wanted to have a memorable trip to somewhere they had never been, and wanted to talk to someone with experience to help them. One referral leads to another and, in this case, many referrals!"*

## Property Services Business Categories

Property Services business categories almost always find money on the table when the couple getting married combines households and move in together.

**Cleaning** Do you have someone you can trust to clean your house before and after the wedding?

Are you having the carpet cleaned before your future in-laws arrive?

**Furniture Sales** Do you know someone who can find furniture that expresses who you are as a couple at a great price for the new household?

**General Contractor** Do you have a general contractor you can trust to convert unused space into a state-of-the-art home office?

### *Joel Zanoff* – *General Contractor: "One House, Two Home Offices"*

*"We've worked with several married couples who were moving into one or the other's home and who needed more space, particularly office space. In these cases, they both worked from home at least a few days a week and both needed their computer space, so we've taken bedrooms and put in some built-ins for desk areas.*

*Same with basements, we finish off basements and create some outstanding office space! I bring in the electrician from my group for cabling all their computers and networking them together. And that's business for another networking partner, because it creates a good referral for the computer pro in my networking group, as well."*

**Interior Design** Do you have a resourceful interior designer to help mix two households of furniture and art, as well as save money on new furniture and accessories?

**Landscaping** Do you have a good landscaper to take care of your home's exterior so you have more time to enjoy your new life together?

**Security Systems** Do you have a home security system to protect your new spouse and home against burglary and fire, as well as save money on your homeowner's insurance?

## Real Estate/Finance Business Categories

From financial planning to buying a new home, people in the Real Estate/ Finance Contact Sphere often find money on the table when a couple is getting married.

**Attorney (Business)** Do you have a good attorney to create a Will or a Trust to protect your new spouse?

**CPA** Do you have a CPA you can trust for tax planning and preparation as a married couple?

**Financial Planner** Do you have someone you can trust to help you make smart investments for your retirement and a college fund if you decide to have children?

---

*John Chichester* – Financial Planning : "Two People, One Financial Plan"

*"A couple I've been working with for several years referred me to their daughter, who is in her 20s and had a sizable trust left to her by her grandmother.*

*The daughter has been a client of mine now for two or three years and is planning to get married. Her fiancé is an attorney and has his own financial planner. We had a big conversation and we talked about her investments, we talked about her asset allocations, and generally where she is financially. Up to now they have been running their finances separately, and they now need to bring those together. Whether it's me or the person he is working with, one of us is going to have to help them get all of their finances on the same page."*

**Insurance** Do you have a good insurance agent to protect your new spouse with life, health and disability insurance?

**Mortgages** Do you have a knowledgeable mortgage officer who can help you take some equity out of your house to pay for the wedding and honeymoon?

**Realtor** Do you have an experienced Realtor who can help you sell or rent one of your houses or buy a new home together?

---

*Kristie Smith – Realtor: "One Wedding, Three Transactions"*

*"I am working with a couple planning to get married. They both own homes and want to sell both homes and buy a new home together. Moving in together is a really special thing for them.*

*Managing these clients has been very interesting because the wedding preparation already has so much stress that the process of buying and selling their homes could be overwhelming. We decided to wait until after the ceremony and the three-week honeymoon, to start the process, which is where we are now.*

*They decided to move into her property, where they are now living, and we are now working to find a new property. We did sell her home quickly and it will be closing soon. If we don't find the new property in time, they will move into his house, but ideally, we could find something new for them to move into and then sell his property."*

## *Wellness Business Categories*

Getting married is a life-changing event. Couples always want to look their best and feel healthy as they put money on the table for your Power Team partners in the Wellness Contact Sphere.

**Chiropractor** Do you have a good chiropractor to help ease your aches and pains so you can be at your best for the wedding and honeymoon?

**Life Coach** Are you working with an experienced life coach for pre-marital counseling?

---

*Judith Joyce – Journey Beyond Belief – Life Coach: "Marriage Counseling"*

*"I work with couples before they get married. It starts with a questionnaire each completes individually, and has questions about what drew them together, their perspectives on money, communication, decision-making, a variety of life issues that can be problematic and dramatically affect a relationship.*

Almost all couples, even those who are already married, benefit from training and working with a life coach who can help them better see each other's perspective, and as a result, have a happier and more fulfilling marriage."

**Massage**  Have you thought of giving a gift certificate for a massage to the wedding party, family or bride and groom?

---

*Alina Pellicer, LMT – Massage Therapist: "One Wedding, Six Massages"*

"A lot of my referrals happen when one neighbor tells another about me and then they become a client. My client's daughter was getting married and hired me for the day before the wedding to work on herself, her daughter, her bridesmaids and another friend. I went to her house and did six massages that day!"

**Nutrition**  Are you taking the best nutritional products to help you lose weight and feel great for the wedding?

**Personal Trainer**  Do you know a personal trainer to help you lose weight and get in great shape for the wedding and honeymoon?

**Water Treatment**  Do you know a water quality professional to make sure you and your new spouse are drinking, cooking and also showering in clean, healthy water?

---

*Brian McCowin – McCowin Enterprises: "Water Treatment for Newlyweds"*

"We have a whole-house water treatment system that quite a few couples getting married invest in. One couple in particular just got married and bought a house and the water softener was something that was really important to them. It cuts the cost of cleaning products way down, but more importantly it usually doubles or triples the life of the big home appliances like the clothes washer or dryer, as well as the water heater and even the pipes. It also takes a lot of the impurities out of the water, including chlorine, which makes it a lot better to drink, is easier on your skin, and is just all-around better for you."

# Chapter 16

# *Relocation 36+ Referrals*

**P**eople moving into or out of town are a targeted prospect for most businesses, spanning all six of the Contact Spheres.

Let's focus on recognizing the Relocation Key Situation as the first step in the sequence of creating referrals.

## *"Relocation" Target Market's Basic Needs*

People relocating to a new area have an almost unlimited range of needs and challenges creating referral possibilities for virtually all of the business categories on your Power Team.

## *Referrals to an Assortment of Industries*

*Beth M. Anderson – BethMAnderson.com : "Relocation Referral Bonanza"*

*"We had a couple who got transferred into town. He was the manager of a chain of home improvement stores and didn't know anybody, but he knew about BNI. His wife is a hairdresser and she joined our networking group. She was able to work with the mortgage officer and the Realtor, because they were renting until they figured out where they wanted to live.*

*As a hairdresser, she wound up passing a lot of referrals back and forth with the massage therapist. She rented a chair at a local salon and worked with the promotional products person to promote her business, as well as the printer in our group for cards, letterhead and all that, in addition to advertising in a "Shopper" mail out they do, both for the hairdressing business and the home improvement store, which turned into a big account for the printer.*

*The banker in the group not only got their personal accounts, but they transferred over their business accounts, as well. The husband had aspirations to continue moving up the corporate ladder with the store chain, so he worked with the business coach in our group to help him do that. The accountant started doing their bookkeeping and tax accounting. Once they got into their new house, he started working with our local insurance agent and unfortunately they had a big plumbing problem so they were able to pull in Mr. Rooter Plumbing to take care of that.*

*Over the course of two years or so, it must have turned into business for a dozen or more people in our group. In fact, they were only in town for a couple of years. The husband got his big promotion, and moved to a bigger store, so again the Realtor was able to sell the house, and the contractor also had work."*

## Trigger Questions

Regardless of your business category, once you identify that someone you meet or already know is in the Relocation Key Situation, you begin asking questions to uncover a need your Power Team can solve.

*Because they have so many needs, simply asking "What is your biggest challenge right now with the move?" will open a floodgate of referrals.*

Now you have the prospect talking and you must listen carefully. Do you have a Power Team partner who can be of service? Continue asking questions to uncover a need. Here are Relocation Key Solution follow up trigger questions and success stories for 36 popular business categories.

# Business Services

Most people moving into or out of town will be involved with a business as either an owner or employee. Many will need help transitioning a home office or primary business location.

**Computers** Do you have a computer pro to get rid of any computer viruses, set up a home office, or just send digital photos and videos of your new location to friends and family over the Internet?

**Office Machines** Will you need a fax or copier for your new home office?

**Printing** Do you have a good, reliable printer for business forms, cards, letterhead and promotional materials in your new location?

**Promotional Products** Have you thought about refrigerator magnets with your new address and local phone number to send to friends and family back home and around the country?

**Telecommunications** Do you and your family have a reliable and affordable Family Minute Plan with a local phone number?

Are you using VOIP (Voice Over Internet Phone) to save on long distance telephone bills at home and work?

**Thank You Gifts** There are a lot of people who have helped you out during this move. Have you found a local gift basket company you can trust for all of your gifting needs?

# Events Business Categories

"Going away," "bon voyage" and "open house" or "house warming" parties are common big events for the Relocation Key Situation.

**Caterer** Have you found a caterer for a special house warming/going-away party who makes great food, gives friendly service and is very reliable?

---

### Ralph Swagler – *Catering: "Long-Distance Client, Local Referral"*

*"We had clients who were moving here from Oregon and were going to get married here. They asked some friends who lived here to put together a short list of local caterers, which they did, and the people actually met with all the caterers and sampled their food, and picked us to work with.*

*In catering, when you meet people for the first time, it's about professionalism, from following up on referrals to finishing the job. Whenever we are given a referral, it's an immediate follow-up. We don't put things off for a day or two, or a week to see what's going to happen. As soon as the referral comes in, we jump on it. It's very important. Even if you are referred and very good at what you do, if you don't move quickly you may lose the job to a competitor."*

**Event Planner** Are you getting stressed trying to plan your house warming/going-away party yourself or do you have a professional event planner to make sure everything goes right so you can enjoy the event?

Have you thought of working with an experienced event planner for an open-house party to meet your neighbors and their friends in your new location?

**Florist** Do you have a florist you can trust to make everything beautiful at your house warming/going-away party?

---

### Sheri Cervantes – Florist : "Welcome Home Gift"

*"I get a lot of business related to people moving into a new home. That is always a great time to send a nice plant or flower arrangement. It's kind of like a sign of growth for something that is new for them, so it's always nice to give them something that will grow along with them in their new home!"*

**Jeweler** Are you working with an experienced jeweler to create a beautiful piece of jewelry for a special neighbor, school teacher or someone else as a "going away" gift? Have you met a good jeweler in your new location who can clean and fix your jewelry, as well as thinking ahead for the next gift you would like to give (or receive).

**Limousine Service** Have you made arrangements with a reputable limo service with professional drivers you can trust to be safe and reliable to transport VIPs to and from the house warming/going-away party?

**Photographer** Are you working with an experienced, professional photographer to capture the memories of your house warming/going-away party?

---

### Tani Dugger –Insight Photography: "Photo Memories of Home"

*"I had some clients who love their house, but they know they may not stay there forever. When I went to their house to take their portraits they wanted to show more of the house as opposed to just them. So we did some shots on the outside, in the backyard, and the front of the house as well. They really liked their house and they wanted to document that period of their lives."*

## *Personal Services Business Categories*

People moving into town always need recommendations to a wide variety of local products and services.

**Auto Repair** Do you have a good auto mechanic in your new location you can trust to keep your family vehicles safe and reliable?

**Errands/Delivery** Do you have someone in your new location you can count on to pick up groceries and run errands while you are trying to set up your new home or office in a new location?

**Greeting Cards**  Do you have an easy-to-use, computer-based greeting card system to mail top-quality "Change of Address" cards in your own handwriting, with the option of including photos as well, for friends, family, clients, prospects, referral sources and vendors?

---

*Nathan Dominguez* – BNI Arizona and Send Out Cards:
*"Change of Address Cards"*

*"Change of Address cards are great for business or personal use. If your company or friends are going to keep in touch with you, they need to know how. You can very easily create a greeting card campaign and send it to your entire database in a matter of minutes, letting them know what your new address will be and when you will be there."*

**Pet Services**  Do you have someone you can trust for dog walks and empty house visits in your new location so your pets will always be cared for?

---

*Kevin McClure* – Leashes and Leads, Pet Services: *"Old Friends in New Places"*

*"We have a lot of people who are new in town and need to have their pets cared for or boarded while they are getting settled in. We give a lot of tours of our facility, which we are very proud of, so they can see where their pet will be staying. We also require that all pets be current with all vaccinations, which is very important. People know when they leave their pet with us they don't have to worry. In many cases, these customers find value in our training classes. We have new puppy classes, obedience and agility training classes, and many more."*

**Personal Chef**  Do you have a personal chef to make sure you and your spouse eat healthy, home-cooked meals in your new location?

---

*Mary Ellen Rae* – Personal Touch Gourmet : *"New Home Holiday"*

*"One of my networking partners referred me to their mom who was moving into town and she wanted to host Thanksgiving dinner in this big, beautiful home they had just purchased. The daughter suggested that instead of trying to do all the work herself, the mom should call me to do a Drop-Off Dinner service instead.*

*The mom called me, we worked out the menu and I took care of all the details. I prepared the meal in my kitchen, brought it to them hot, made-to-order and ready-to-eat. That was a lot of fun for me, and it really helped the people who were new in town and not yet set up to entertain to enjoy a family holiday with a Thanksgiving dinner for eight in their new home."*

**Travel Agent** Have you taken advantage of the experience and discount pricing of a professional travel agent who can save you money for a much-deserved vacation after the move?

## Property Services Business Categories

Similar to Personal Services, people working in Property Service Contact Sphere business categories have a lot of money on the table with the Relocation Key Situation.

**Cleaning** Do you have someone you can trust to clean your new house before you move in?

Do you have a cleaning service for your air conditioning ducts and the best filters to make sure you and your family are breathing clean, healthy air inside your new home?

**Furniture Sales** Do you know someone who can find the right furniture for your new home at a great price?

**General Contractor** Do you need a licensed general contractor to build a home or office building from the ground up or for repairs and remodels?

---

*Joel Zanoff* –*General Contractor: "Fix Up, Move Out"*

*"I do a fair amount of repairs for presentation, as we say, before a property is put on the market to be sold, where we go in and it may be as little as painting a room and putting up some crown molding. If there's rotted wood on the house, we repair that, too. Nobody wants to buy a house that has rotten trim and exterior problems."*

**Interior Design** Do you have a talented and resourceful interior designer to help make your new home beautiful, safe and functional, as well as save money on new furniture and accessories?

**Landscaping** Do you have a reliable landscaper in your new location to make your lawn, plants and trees stay healthy and beautiful?

**Security Systems** Do you have a home security system to protect your family in your new home and save money on your homeowner's insurance?

*James Hamilton – ADT Security Systems:*
*"The Insurance Broker and Proactive Habits"*

*"Daniel Jacoby in Chapter 37 in Manhattan is a super insurance broker who has given me so much work, I can't tell you how grateful I am to him. He specializes in property and casualty insurance and I get about one referral a week from him that turns into closed business.*

*He makes it a habit to proactively tell people, "By the way, we have a partnership with one of the ADT Security System Dealerships here in town and you should give him a call if you want to save money on your insurance and protect your home at the same time."*

## *Real Estate/Finance Business Categories*

Realtors, mortgage and insurance business categories thrive on the Relocation Key Situation. Along with the local CPA, financial planner and attorney, these businesses are dealing with people in transition on a regular basis, creating money on the table for the rest of the Power Team.

**Attorney (Business)** Do you have a good attorney in your new location for any business or legal matters you may need help with?

**CPA** Do you have a good CPA in your new location you can trust to save money on tax planning and preparation?

**Financial Planner** Do you have someone in your new location you can trust to help you make smart investments for a college fund and your retirement?

**Insurance** Do you have a good insurance agent in your new location to protect your new home and save money by combining coverage with your auto policy?

*Mike McKee –Andrews & McKee Insurance:*
*"Coast to Coast Insurance Referrals"*

*"People moving into town are a big source of business for us. A lot of that is education on the laws and rules here in Minnesota, as well as why rates are different here as opposed to where they are from. People generally need to have their homeowner's and auto insurance changed for the new location, and a lot of times any health insurance they have also needs to be looked at.*

*For folks moving out of town, we are licensed in certain states, so many times I can help them by simply changing and updating their policy if we are licensed where they are going. If not, I can refer them to someone they can trust to make sure they get the coverage they need.*

*People really like to know that they are working with someone they can trust to be sure they are getting the coverage they need at a fair price and just in general, that they are not being taken advantage of by someone they've never met."*

**Mortgages**  Do you have a knowledgeable mortgage officer in your new location to help with the mortgage loan for your new home?

**Realtor**  Do you have an experienced Realtor who can not only help you get the right house at the best possible price, but also help with your family's transition into a new community?

---

### Kristie Smith – Realtor : "Service Before and After the Sale"

*"One of the things I do is help local corporations move their executive transferees to the local area. A lot of times, I even get involved during the recruiting process. So it starts as a partnership with a local company, maybe a local hospital, for example, who wants to hire a Physician, or a Vice President or a Director.*

*Most transferees are not just interviewing and trying to figure out "Do I want to work for this company?" They are also wondering, "Do I want to move to Indiana?" I get involved during the interview process and help sell the city to the potential employee. Everything from art, entertainment, education, cost of living, what our traffic is like. It seems well received because I am a third-party vendor. I'm not the recruiter trying to recruit the person, so I can offer another perspective.*

*Many times, I'll get involved with the trailing spouse and help that spouse feel comfortable about the area, opportunities for their children, what kind of house can they really get for the money. Or a trailing spouse may need job placement assistance or need to network in their field if they have some sort of specialty. So if the wife is an IT person or the husband is in a particular field, I can connect them with what we call Trailing Spouse Networking and actually help them land a position.*

*Once the person accepts the job, I really change hats and become the relocation real estate expert, I'm no longer helping seal the deal for the job, the company has hired the person. At that point, I'm now putting all their real estate needs into motion.*

*We have done everything from move horses across the country for people to transporting cars, and we always make sure a good mover is going to take care of their property."*

## Wellness Business Categories

Establishing a good relationship with local experts in the Wellness Contact Sphere is very important, and in some cases critical, to people moving into a new town.

**Chiropractor**  Do you have a good chiropractor in your new location to ease your aches and pains?

**Life Coach**  Are you working with an experienced life coach in your new location to help you and your family adjust to all the challenges of moving to a new location?

---

*Judith Joyce* –Journey Beyond Belief – Life Coach: "Three-Stage Transition"

*"Moving is obviously a big transition. First we look at what they feel they are losing, which is a sort of "grieving" phase, but then we also look at all the things they've received from the place and people they are leaving. These are things they can take with them that can help them create a good situation in their new place.*

*The second phase can be viewed as a "field of all possibilities," where you've got one foot in the old place, one foot in the new place, but there's still a lot of things you do during that time to focus on the things you'd like to create in your new location.*

*And then there's the new beginning, which can be very exciting. Helping people see things from a different perspective, focusing on opportunities they might be overlooking and supporting them as they bring together the other phases of the experience into building their new life."*

**Massage**  Do you have an experienced massage therapist in your new location to help maintain optimal health and feel great?

*Alina Pellicer, LMT – Massage Therapist: "New in Town"*

*"When I hear of someone new in town, I always ask them if they have found a variety of other healing modalities, things that are related to my business in massage, like a chiropractor or a naturopathic doctor. So we get to talking about a lot of different things and I start handing out cards.*

*I always make it a point to tell my clients that these are people from my networking group whom I know and I trust very much, and if they ever need a referral to someone in any type of situation, things like computers, real estate or repairs around the house, they can call me."*

**Nutrition**   Are you taking the best nutritional products to help you stay healthy with all the stress and strain of moving to a new location?

**Personal Trainer**   Do you know a personal trainer in your new location you can trust to help you lose weight and get in great shape?

**Water Purification**   Do you know a water quality professional in your new location to make sure you and your family are drinking, cooking and also showering in clean, healthy water?

## Chapter 17

# *New Baby 36+ Referrals*

**P**eople expecting a new baby or who already have a newborn are the primary target market for a variety of business categories in the Wellness Contact Sphere.

- Chiropractor
- Life Coach
- Massage
- Nutrition
- Personal Trainer
- Water/Air Treatment

These six wellness business categories are examples of a broader spectrum of products and services aimed at health and wellness.

While helping their clients and customers, people working in these business categories can be trained to find money on the table for your business as well, even if you are not directly or traditionally related to the health and wellness industry.

Focus on recognizing the New Baby Key Situation as the first step in the sequence of creating referrals.

### New Baby Target Market's Basic Needs

- Prenatal and postnatal health care for mom and baby
- Changes to the home
- Time management/help at home
- Financial planning

Real Estate and Finance Contact Spheres are an easy referral for couples planning for the future, securing their investments and buying and selling real estate. In addition, Business, Personal and Property Services Contact Spheres, as well as Events categories, also offer a wide variety of products and services that are frequently of value to a growing household.

## Referrals to Other Industries

---

### Beth M. Anderson – BethMAnderson.com:
#### "Growing Family Creates Referrals"

*"One of the women in my networking group was having her third child and had a lot of trouble with her back, so the massage therapist got a referral. During the massage, she told the massage therapist that they were going to buy a new house, because theirs was a two bedroom. So the massage therapist was able to give her over to the mortgage pro, as well as the Realtor.*

*Women talk to their massage therapist kind of like they do their hairdressers, so she found out more about what was going on in the woman's life and was able to create some great referrals as a result. There were a lot of them. The insurance agent and the financial planner got a referral because they were concerned about the cost of college, the cosmetics representative got a referral for some personal products that the expecting mom needed, the handyman was needed to get the house ready for sale.*

*In fact she also gave a referral to the photographer in the group to take pictures of the mother while she was pregnant. So a lot of different things lead to business revolving around the lifestyle changes that happened with this third child."*

## Trigger Questions

Regardless of your business category, once you identify that someone you meet or already know is expecting a new baby, you begin asking questions to uncover a need your Power Team can solve.

The following trigger questions are fast and effective tools to start turning money on the table into money-making referrals:

- **Congratulations! So, when is the new baby due? Great! So** *what is your biggest challenge with getting ready for the new baby?*

- *Are you having a baby shower?*

- *So, while you are taking care of everything to get ready for the new baby, what else is going on in your life or business right now?*

Now that you have the prospect talking, you must listen carefully. Do you have a Power Team partner who can be of service? Continue asking questions to uncover a need. Here are New Baby Key Situation follow-up trigger questions and success stories to help you create referrals for 36 popular business categories.

## *Business Services*

People in the New Baby Key Situation often are also in business, either as an owner or employee, creating "traditional" referrals for Business Services categories. In addition, some of these products and services can be specifically targeted to the arrival of the new baby.

**Telecommunications** Do you and your spouse have a reliable and affordable Family Minute Plan?

**Computers** Do you have a computer pro to help you send digital photos and videos of the new baby to friends and family over the Internet?

**Business Coaching** Do you and your spouse use a business coach for personal development, communication and time management skills to adjust to life with the new baby and balancing work and family?

**Printing** Do you have a good, reliable printer for extra special new baby announcements or invitations to the Christening?

**Promotional Products** Have you thought of making personalized "It's a Boy" or "It's a Girl" cigars or baby announcement refrigerator magnets?

---

*Patrick Finley* –Art Promotional Services, LLC: "Baby Announcement Magnets"

*"A friend of mine and his wife were having a baby and when it came time to do the baby announcements, I talked to him and said, "Wouldn't you rather send out a hundred magnets to tell all your friends and family that your baby was born?" He took the idea to his wife and they ran with it. The magnets worked out great! We had a picture, the*

*birthday, as well as the baby's weight and length. People are going to put the announcement on the refrigerator anyway, so why not do it on a magnet?"*

**Thank You Gifts** Have you seen those adorable "Diaper Cake" centerpieces? I know a local gift basket company that can create a custom-designed centerpiece for your baby shower. Do you have a really great gift for the people who attend the baby shower? A custom gift basket would make a great thank-you gift for your shower host and hostess.

## Events Business Categories

Asking prospects for the New Baby Key Situation, "Are you planning a baby shower?" will uncover money on the table for the Events business categories.

**Caterer** Have you found a caterer for the baby shower who makes great food, gives friendly service and is very reliable?

**Event Planner** Are you getting stressed trying to plan everything yourself or do you have a professional event planner to make sure everything goes right so you can enjoy your baby shower?

**Florist** Do you have a florist you can trust to make everything beautiful at your baby shower?

---

### Sheri Cervantes – Florist : "Flowers for Baby Showers"

*"A client of mine who was pregnant was referred to me by the property and casualty insurance person in my networking group. She wanted to order flowers for the baby shower. I made the phone call, got the job and it turned out great. The feedback was that everybody was ecstatic over the design of the flower arrangements. That led to some of the family members calling me for flowers to send to the new mom when the baby arrived. I guess you could say it was a "chain reaction" referral!"*

**Jeweler** Are you working with an experienced jeweler to create a beautiful "Push Gift" to commemorate the big day for the new mom to treasure forever?

---

### Morris Esses – Jeweler: "Push Gift"

*"My sales people are always recommending "Push Gifts" to expectant fathers. One really good customer of ours, who had purchased an engagement ring, came looking for something to celebrate the coming birth of his and his wife's first child. My salesperson showed him a*

beautiful diamond necklace. We made him a great deal on it, and he left a deposit."

The day after the baby was born, he came rushing in, and told us the good news. He showed us a picture of the baby on his telephone and he picked up the necklace. Before the mom even came home from the hospital with the baby, he had this beautiful necklace to give her.

She came in a couple of months later with the baby, strolling along, and she told us how impressed she was by it, how much she loved it and how important a gift it was to her. So a Push Gift really does have an impact on a relationship and it's something that a wife really, really enjoys!"

**Limousine Service**  Have you made arrangements with a reputable limo service for the trip to the hospital?

---

### Joe Greco – Limousine Service: "Deliver in Style"

"There are several reasons someone having a baby should use a limousine service to get to the hospital and then back home with the new baby in the car, and a big one is convenience. We provide door to door service and also help with the luggage and anything else they might be carrying. We help them in and out of the car, hold doors open for them and make sure they have no inconvenience.

Plus our vehicles are extremely clean and very reliable. We clean and safety check our cars every day. New moms and dads appreciate that type of service when bringing a new baby home from the hospital."

**Photographer**  Are you working with an experienced, professional photographer to capture the memories of your new baby and young family?

---

### Tani Dugger – Insight Photography: "Pregnancy Photos"

"I do pregnancy pictures. Unlike back in the '50s when women tried to hide their bellies when they were pregnant, women now celebrate their bellies. A lot of women even have plaster molds made of them. The women love the pictures and I believe it helps the fathers be a little more involved in the pregnancy, because I certainly encourage the fathers to join in the session.

I also photograph the birth, as well. I was at a home birth and I could see the tension in the father waiting as the baby was being born, so I turned and photographed him. You could see the tension and stress in *his face and as soon as the baby was okay, and took its first breath, you could just see the relief on his face. In the multiple images, I captured exactly how that happened, and I think they will cherish those photos forever."*

## *Personal Services Business Categories*

Bringing a new baby into the home requires a lot of preparation and changes many of the family's regular routines, creating money-making referrals for the Personal Services categories.

**Auto Repair** Do you have a good, honest auto mechanic you can trust to keep your family vehicles safe and reliable?

**Errands/Delivery** Do you have someone you can count on to pick up groceries and run errands while the new mom is recovering from the birth?

---

*Lauren Chandler* –*SGI Solutions, Delivery and Errand Service:*
*"Special Delivery"*

*"We got a phone call from a woman whose daughter was having a baby, but couldn't be there with her. So, the mother called a florist to order a big arrangement, plus a big basket, and, for some reason, the florist couldn't deliver it, so, she wanted us to pick up the items from the florist, along with a couple of knickknacks that she had already called and paid for, from another store, including a cake. She wanted us to pick all that stuff up and deliver it to her daughter. She really appreciated the fact that we could get that done for her!"*

**Greeting Cards** Do you have an easy-to-use, computer-based greeting card system to mail top-quality baby announcements in your own handwriting, with the option of including photos to friends and family?

---

*Nathan Dominguez* – *BNI Arizona and Send Out Cards:*
*"New Baby Announcement"*

*"When my wife was pregnant, we sent out greeting cards in a couple of stages. The first was when we found out she was pregnant with an announcement, "The Dominguez family is growing!"*

*After our son was born, we sent out cards with his smiling beautiful face on the front, with a blue border announcing the weight and size. Since then we've also used greeting cards for birthday party invitations, just* about any kind of announcement we can think of. Putting the photos into the card makes it fun. It's so easy to do and the people who get the greeting card in the mail really hang on to it!"

**Pet Services** Do you have someone you can trust for dog walks and empty house visits while mom recovers from giving birth or when you go on vacation?

---

*Kevin McClure – Leashes and Leads, Pet Services:*
*"Dog Walks and New Baby Training"*

*"I know that when we had our baby about a year and a half ago, the last thing we wanted to do when we came home from the hospital, and especially when we were in the hospital, was worry about feeding the dog and taking the dog for a walk. We just had other things, like the baby, on our minds at that time.*

*So we can take the pet in either for the day or boarding, and then reintroduce the pet into the home with the new baby in the picture. That's a good time frame for training, with dogs being very territorial and protective, our trainers can spend some time with them and their pet to adjust to having a little one at home."*

**Personal Chef** Do you have a personal chef to make sure you and your spouse eat healthy, home cooked meals while the new mom is recovering from giving birth?

---

*Mary Ellen Rae –Personal Touch Gourmet: "New Moms Need Help!"*

*"New moms need help preparing meals at home. I've worked with lots of new moms. Many times they have other small kids, they are overwhelmed and exhausted. Sometimes new moms can't physically cook for themselves or their family and it saves the husband, who is also usually on overload from having to step in and do the cooking."*

**Travel Agent** Have you taken advantage of the experience and discount pricing of a professional travel agent who can save you money and make sure you have a great time on your first vacation with the new baby?

## Property Services Business Categories

Bringing a new baby into the home requires a lot of preparation and changes many of the family's regular responsibilities and routines, creating money-making referrals for the Property Services categories.

**Cleaning** Do you have someone you can trust to clean your house and carpets before the baby arrives and while the new mother is recovering from giving birth?

Do you have a professional cleaning company to clean the air-conditioning ducts and install the best filters to make sure you, your spouse and especially the new baby are breathing clean, healthy air inside your home?

**Furniture Sales** Do you know someone who can find the right baby furniture at a great price?

**General Contractor** Do you need a licensed general contractor you can trust to build an addition to your home or do some remodeling to create a safe and healthy place for the new baby?

---

*Joel Zanoff* –*General Contractor: "Safe for Baby"*

*"We've done a lot of room conversions for clients taking a home office and turning it into a baby's room. We've also done a lot of baby-proofing for people, putting up gates on stairs and baby-proof electric outlets, as well as handles and locks on kitchen and bathroom cabinets."*

**Interior Design** Do you have a talented and resourceful interior designer to help make your home safe and functional for the arrival of the new baby, as well as save money on furniture and accessories for the baby nursery?

**Landscaping** Do you have a reliable landscaper to make sure your landscaping is safe for children to play outside and who can also take care of your home's exterior so you have more time for your growing family?

**Security Systems** Do you have a home security system to protect your home and growing family against burglary and fire, as well as the new baby with a carbon monoxide alarm, a "Nanny Cam" and good intercoms?

## Real Estate/Finance Business Categories

Expectant parents are usually so busy with the health of the mom and new baby, as well as the day-to-day logistics of getting the house and everything else ready, they often forget or are too busy to take care of insurance and financial planning. Although it may take a little prodding, the New Baby Key Situation puts a lot of money on the table for the Real Estate and Finance Contact Sphere.

**Attorney** Do you have a good attorney to create a Will or a Trust to protect both spouses and new baby?

**CPA** Do you have a CPA you can trust for tax planning and preparation as a growing family?

**Financial Planner** Do you have someone you can trust to help you make smart investments for a college fund and your retirement?

---

### John Chichester –Financial Planning:
#### "New Babies, College and Estate Planning"

"I was given a referral from an acupuncturist who was meeting with a young couple expecting a baby. We ended up doing a financial plan for them. One of their biggest concerns was college education. So we built in funding at the start of the plan for their child's college education. It's interesting, because they are also doctors, so did a full financial plan for their medical practice.

But their initial thing was, "We're pregnant, we have a new business, we're doing well and making good money, but we don't really know what we are supposed to be doing with it."

They had no estate plan. No plan for a guardian after the child was born, so we got with an estate planning attorney to make sure they got that all sewn up.

In fact, they just had baby number two about six months ago, and immediately, their first thing was to get everything in order. They just feel better knowing they have a good handle on their financial future and security for their family."

**Insurance** Do you have a good insurance agent to protect your spouse and new baby with life, health and disability insurance?

---

### Beth M. Anderson –BethMAnderson.com: "New Babies and Life Insurance"

"I got my homeowner's and auto insurance from the insurance agent in my networking group and that came about because I referred myself to her. After we sat down for our first one-to-one meeting outside the group I asked her about her passions and she told me a story about life insurance from her personal history and why she got into selling insurance.

It turns out that she has a passion for seeing that young families get life insurance. She told me a story about a young man who died in a car accident and his wife was able to carry on without financial woes because they had just bought life insurance on him. That made me realize just how important these insurance products are and I am always on the lookout for her, whenever I come in contact with couples having a baby. It is a definite trigger for me."

### Mike McKee –Andrews & McKee Insurance:
#### "Beyond Life Insurance – Health and Disability"

"It's time for people to take out life insurance when there's a baby on the way. Same with health and disability insurance. I always ask about what would happen if something happened to the breadwinner and the other spouse has to go out and work. Not only do you have the loss of income, but there are a lot of other expenses, things like day care for the baby, that need to be managed.

Nothing means more to a parent than the well-being of their child and, of course, their spouse. It's easy to procrastinate with insurance, so I always try to get the people in my networking group to mention me when they talk to someone who is having a baby."

**Mortgages** Do you have a knowledgeable mortgage officer who can help you take some equity out of your house to pay for any home improvements you need before the new baby arrives?

**Realtor** Do you have an experienced Realtor who can help you purchase a larger home for your growing family as well as sell or rent one of the houses you are in now?

### Kristie Smith –Realtor: "Growing Families and Referral Relationships"

"We really view a new birth as a huge event in our business. Typically, the new baby does not initiate a sale right away. People usually need time to figure all that out. One of the things we do is send out a new baby gift whenever we hear about a baby being born from one of our clients. Client, friend, neighbor, I always send a gift when I get the opportunity.

I use it as a referral opportunity, because one of the people in my networking group makes these really neat baby gifts.

*I recently worked with a couple who purchased their very first home with me about five years ago, and they had two children while living there. They were ready to move to a bigger house. When their second child was eight months old they contacted me, and although their house had been a little bit destroyed by the kids, we got the house ready for sale. It actually took about three months and we used a lot of the people from my networking group.*

*We sold the house in four days and now they are purchasing a new home that needs quite a bit of work. The whole sequence of events started because of the growing family. We sent baby gifts to each of their two children when they were born, built a nice relationship over time and kept in touch. They've given me so many referrals over the years and have been major referral partners for me, as well as a lot of the people in my networking group."*

## *Wellness Business Categories*

New babies create an abundance of money-making referrals for the Wellness Contact Sphere business categories.

**Chiropractor**  Do you have a good prenatal chiropractor to help ease the expecting new mom's aches and pains during the pregnancy?

**Life Coach**  Are you working with an experienced life coach to help you and your spouse prepare for the many challenges that will come up as your family grows?

---

*Judith Joyce* –Journey Beyond Belief – Life Coach: "Parenting Styles"

*"Differences of opinion around a parenting style can cause a lot of problems in the home. Working with a life coach on those issues in advance, or even after the baby is born, can make a huge difference in helping the parents really understand each other and work much more effectively together as a team, rather than constantly butting heads on all the little day-to-day decisions around parenting."*

**Massage**  Do you have an experienced prenatal massage therapist who specializes in pregnant women and new babies?

### Lisa D. Rossi, LMT – Massage Therapy: "Massage for Mom"

*A wife of one of the guys in my networking group was pregnant with her third baby and I started working with her about seven months into her pregnancy. I saw her once a week and she felt like her back was completely better than it had been during her previous two pregnancies. She also had a very smooth delivery, which she attributed to working with me.*

**Nutrition** Are you taking the best nutritional products for the baby's health and to help you feel great for the baby's birth?

**Personal Trainer** Do you know a personal trainer you can trust to help the new mom be physically prepared for giving birth, as well as to help you lose weight and get into great shape after the baby is born?

**Water Treatment** Do you know a water quality professional to make sure the new baby, as well as you and your spouse, are drinking, cooking, bathing, and also showering in clean, healthy water?

### Brian McCowin – McCowin Enterprises:
#### "New Babies, Sensitive Skin and Healthy Water"

*"We have clients with new babies who are proactive and concerned about the tap water in their area. So we ended up putting in reverse osmosis water filtration systems so they can make their baby formula, as well as make it safe for bathing the baby.*

*I had a couple of clients whose babies were having terrible rashes and it turned out that the chlorine levels in the tap water was high, so we put in a system to remove the chlorine and soften up the water. It worked well and cleared up the baby's rash within a week!"*

# Chapter 18

# *Real Estate 36+ Referrals*

There are various types of Real Estate Key Situations that put money on the table for your networking group:

- Buying
- Selling
- Building/New Construction
- Remodeling
- Maintaining
- Managing

People in Real Estate Key Situations are the primary target market for Property Services and Real Estate/Finance Contact Spheres.

| **Property Services** | **Real Estate / Finance** |
|---|---|
| ▪ Cleaning Service | ▪ Attorney |
| ▪ Furniture Sales | ▪ CPA |
| ▪ General Contractor | ▪ Financial Planner |
| ▪ Interior Designer | ▪ Insurance |
| ▪ Landscaper | ▪ Mortgage |
| ▪ Security System | ▪ Realtor |

These twelve business categories are examples of a broader spectrum of products and services aimed at helping people who are in Real Estate Key Situations.

While helping their clients and customers, these business categories can be trained to find money on the table for your business as well, even if you are not directly or traditionally related to the real estate industry.

Focus on recognizing the Real Estate Key Situation as the first step in the networking sequence.

## "Real Estate" Target Market's Basic Needs

- Financial products and real estate brokerage services to buy, sell or lease property

- Contracting services for new construction or remodeling existing property

- Vendors to manage and maintain property

## Referrals to Other Industries

People experiencing a Real Estate Key Situation almost always have other related needs that your Power Team can solve. Learn as much as you can about your networking partners' products and services, as well as what makes him or her special as a person. When opportunity in the form of a Real Estate Key Situation presents itself, ask a few trigger questions. You will be amazed at how much money on the table you will find!

## Trigger Questions

Regardless of your business category, once you identify that someone you meet or already know is in a Real Estate Key Situation, you begin asking questions to uncover a need your Power Team can solve.

The following trigger questions are fast and effective tools to start turning money on the table into money-making referrals:

- *So, how is everything going with your real estate project? What's the biggest challenge right now?"*

- *So, in addition to getting all this real estate stuff done, what's the next big event coming up for you?"*

- *So, in addition to getting all this real estate stuff done, what's the biggest challenge for you these days?"*

Now that you have the prospect talking you must listen carefully. Do you have a Power Team partner who can be of service? Continue asking questions to uncover a need. Here are Real Estate Key Situation follow up trigger questions and success stories to give you ideas to create referrals for 36 popular business categories.

# Business Services

Business Services are an obvious fit for the Real Estate Key Situations.

**Telecommunications**  Have you checked into saving money on your cell phone, texting and handheld Internet?

**Computers**  Do you have a reliable and knowledgeable computer pro to set up the computer network in your new or remodeled home?

Do you have a good computer pro to help you set up software to manage the progress and budget of your new construction project?

**Office Machines**  Are you getting the best price and service on your copier and other office machines for your new or remodeled home office?

**Printing**  Do you have a printer who can make good copies of all those large blueprints you are using for construction or remodeling?

Do you have promotional banners to bring attention to your next open house or grand opening?

**Promotional Products**  Do you have a really sharp promotional products person who can match the right promotional item at the right price to reach your specific real estate target market?

Have you thought about customized calendar magnets, pens, coffee mugs or other promotional products to help your real estate clients remember you?

**Thank You Gifts**  Do you have a great way to thank your clients after a transaction?

*Sample*: "I realize there is a lot of stress in your life right now with all the real estate stuff you are doing, and working with a trusted local gift basket company for all of your gifting needs can certainly help take the stress out of saying "Thank You" to everyone who has helped you along the way!"

*Jenifer Anseth – M.R. Designs & Gifts:*
*"Commercial Furniture and a Grand Opening Two-fer"*

*"I have a Power Team partner who is in commercial furniture sales and after he finishes furnishing an office he likes to send one of our gift baskets for the office's grand opening. From my standpoint, he not only does something to promote his company, but he creates an "in" for me with the new company as well. He also promotes me to the other sales people he works with for their grand openings. I can't begin to tell you how many great referrals he has given me!"*

# Events Business Categories

Events Contact Sphere business categories come into play for celebrating the completion of a real estate project with an open house, grand opening or other special event.

**Caterer** Do you have a caterer who makes great food, gives friendly service and is very reliable for your office open house or grand opening?

Do you have an experienced caterer for a very special open house to promote your high dollar listings?

**Event Planner** Have you thought of working with an experienced event planner for a very special launch event to promote your new real estate product or service?

Have you thought of working with an experienced event planner for a client appreciation party or extra special holiday party to increase the referrals you receive from satisfied real estate clients?

**Florist** Do you have a florist you can trust to bring fresh flowers for the office once a week and also make sure all the plants stay healthy?

**Jeweler** Have you thought of using a "Cash for Gold" service with a local jeweler you can trust to generate some much needed cash flow for your real estate project?

Are you working with an experienced jeweler to create a special piece of jewelry to reward someone who has been particularly helpful in this Real Estate Key Situation?

**Limousine Service** Have you made arrangements with a reputable limo service with professional drivers you can trust to be safe and reliable for rewarding VIP's you've invited to your open house or grand opening?

**Photographer** Are you working with an experienced, professional photographer to take photos of your real estate projects for the Internet and promotional materials?

Are you photographing the various stages of new and existing construction to document the work being done, as well as, "before and after" comparison shots for remodels?

## Personal Services Business Categories

Power Team members in the Personal Services Contact Sphere help people in a Real Estate Key Situation save time, increase convenience and improve their quality of life.

**Auto Repair:** Do you have a good auto mechanic you can trust to keep your company vehicles safe and reliable?

---

### Bill Coniam – 25th Street Automotive: "Old Cars and New Houses"

"A young couple found out about us through the local church. The wife would bring one of their two cars in for an oil change and we helped counsel them over the years. They had an older vehicle and they weren't sure whether or not they were going to keep it, but it was very important to her and her husband that the vehicle be safe.

We advised them on what was best. They ended up not keeping the Chevy for the long run and ultimately shopped for a new vehicle. And that's another service we provide, "Pre Purchase Inspections" for people who want to know if everything is right with the vehicle.

But this couple needed some time before they could buy. We took care of a minor item that was a big concern to buy them some time to get their finances in order while they were closing on their new house. They didn't want to hit their credit with a new car purchase before they had their home, so we bought a little time, they closed on their house and some time after that they got a new car, and we have continued to work on their cars over the years."

**Errands/Delivery** Do you have someone you can count on to pick up/ deliver and run errands while you are busy with your real estate clients or construction crew?

Do you need last-minute or regularly scheduled pick up and delivery of large blueprints or architectural drawings?

Do you need supplies and materials delivered to a job site?

**Greeting Cards**  Do you have an easy-to-use follow-up system for clients, prospects, referral sources and vendors, that lets you mail top-quality greeting cards from your computer with your own handwriting and photos?

---

*Nathan Dominguez – BNI Arizona and Send Out Cards:*
*"Kitchens, Smiles and Following Up"*

*"I have a good friend in real estate who, back during the real estate boom, was selling $1.2 to $2.5 million condos in a great area in Scottsdale. One day a woman walked into the sales office who wanted to look at one of the units, sort of killing time while her husband, a classic-car buff, was at a big car auction. The wife didn't want to look at cars all day, so she was out shopping and looking at real estate.*

*One thing my friend always does is take a camera with her, and as she's showing the home she catches the wife in the kitchen with a big grin on her face standing next to the beautiful granite countertops, and my friend takes a snap shot.*

*After the visitors leave, my friend always sends a follow-up. As always, she sent one to this woman who was in town from California with her husband for the car auction. Basically it was saying thanks for visiting, if you have any interest please let us know and it included a picture of the woman smiling in the kitchen, along with the company logo.*

*About two months later, she gets a call, not from the woman, but the woman's friend. The friend noticed the greeting card at the woman's house. She saw her friend smiling in that beautiful kitchen, and shortly thereafter came out to the sales office and bought a condo for $1.2 million! All that with a follow up card that cost less than a buck."*

**Pet Services**  Do you have someone you can trust for dog walks and empty house visits while you are busy with your Real Estate Key Situation?

---

*Kevin McClure – Leashes and Leads, Pet Services:*
*"Pet Walks While You Work"*

*"Anyone in transition, whether building a new home or displaced because of a fire or remodeling, may need a place for a pet. Also, if they are involved in the construction or are just too busy in general, we can take the dog off their hands so they can just focus on getting the job done."*

**Personal Chef**  Do you have a personal chef to make sure you eat healthy, home-cooked meals at a surprisingly affordable price so you can stay focused on your Real Estate Key Situation?

**Travel Agent**  Have you thought of working with a professional travel agent to create a special "Dream Vacation" as a reward for completing your Real Estate Key Situation?

## Property Services Business Categories

It is easy to be a referral order-taker for your Power Team partners in the Property Services Contact Sphere when you come across someone buying, selling, building, remodeling, maintaining or managing a house or building.

**Cleaning**  Do you have someone you can trust coming to clean the carpets after the remodel to get rid of all the dust from construction?

Do you have someone you can trust to do a one time, or regularly scheduled cleaning?

Do you have a professional cleaner to clean the ducts and use the best air filters to make sure you or the occupants of your property are breathing clean, healthy air?

**Furniture Sales**  Do you know someone who can find great furniture at an affordable price?

**General Contractor**  Do you need any work done to the property that my friend the general contractor can help with?

---

### Joel Zanoff – General Contractor: "Strong Referral Lands Dream Job"

"I got a referral from the lawyer in my network group to remodel a 9,000-square-foot house that belonged to his sister. She and her husband had purchased it and wanted to do a lot of work. We remodeled just about every room in the house, all the bathrooms, all new windows, the kitchen, a lot of electrical and plumbing, and in some cases fixing violations and things that were not done properly. It's been my best referral yet.

The lawyer has seen my work in the past. He's heard testimonials at my networking meeting from other members and I'm sure it was those past testimonials that made him feel comfortable referring me to his sister and her husband. Had it been a cold call or something off an ad, I would have been competing against five other guys who wanted the same job.

*I'm sure he gave a glowing testimonial for me to his sister and said something like, "This is the guy for you! I know him personally and this is the general contractor you want!" I'm sure that's how I got the job."*

**Interior Design**  Do you have a talented and resourceful interior designer to make your new or current home more appealing and operate more efficiently?

Have you thought of bringing in an experienced and talented interior designer to stage your listings so they will sell faster and for more money?

**Landscaping**  Do you have a reliable landscaper to take care of your property's exterior so the plants, shrubs, trees and lawn stay healthy and well maintained?

---

### Taru Fisher – *Personal Fitness: "Email Groups for Leads"*

*"I belong to eWomen Network and Women in Networking and I always go through their Yahoo group emails. One time I came across a woman who was looking to create a backyard garden with water features, by someone who could also rip out the lawn. That was a good referral for the landscaper in my group. I read their Yahoo group emails right away every time I get them to see if there are leads for my group."*

**Security Systems**  Do you have a home security system to protect your new or remodeled home against burglary and fire, as well as save money on your homeowner's insurance?

## Real Estate/Finance Business Categories

Real Estate/Finance Contact Sphere business categories are a no-brainer for money on the table with prospects in a Real Estate Key Situation.

**Attorney (Business)**  Do you have a good attorney to review your business contracts, as well as create a Will or a Trust to protect your assets?

**Attorney (Personal Injury)**  Do you have a good attorney to protect you as a property owner against personal injury lawsuits?

---

### Robert Gross – *Attorney: "Landlord Rights"*

*"I work for people who have been injured, but I also do a lot of work defending companies, and particularly property owners who get sued in cases where people get injured. Sometimes I will ask my network for a referral to a speaking engagement, where I can talk to a trade group*

like the restaurant association, investment property owners or other groups of property and business owners to promote the defense side of my work."

**CPA**  Do you have a CPA you can trust to save money on tax planning and preparation as it relates to your real estate project?

**Financial Planner**  Do you have someone you can trust to help you make smart investments for your retirement, as well as your employees'?

---

### John Chichester – Financial Planning :
#### "More to Investing Than Buying Property"

"I have clients who are real estate people. People with a lot of real estate, not necessarily in the business or as part of their job, but who use real estate as a way to build wealth. What I find is that the only thing they truly understand as an investment is real estate. It's tangible, they can touch it. They are often unfamiliar or unsure of the stock market or mutual funds, or other types of investments. So as a result, they typically just invest back into real estate.

While real estate is very important and an excellent asset to have, it is not the only asset class to have. So what I've done with some of my real estate people is get them to branch out and diversify into some other types of investments that will do well for them in their overall financial plan.

Also, a lot of people who own real estate will own it either outright individually, or inside a corporation, or all owned in one LLC. The problem with that is in the event they get sued, all that can be taken away. So one thing we really work on with my real estate investor clients, is asset and liability protection, which means we structure the ownership of the real estate so that in the event something does happen, they are protected."

---

**Insurance**  Do you have a good insurance agent to protect your property with the best property and casualty insurance for your needs?

---

### Mike McKee – Andrews & McKee Insurance: "Remodel, Revalue, Referral!"

"Last summer a good client of mine did a major remodel job. With homeowner's insurance you've got replacement cost on your dwelling, but there's a clause that says if you remodel and increase the value, you can jeopardize that guaranteed replacement cost. So we had to revalue the house and increase the insurance to make sure that all the new work and improvements would be covered in the event he needed to use the insurance.

On the liability side, when people have a contractor doing a remodel job on their home, I advise them to make sure the contractor has liability coverage by asking the contractor to give them a copy of the Certificate of Insurance to prove they have the coverage."

**Mortgages** Do you have a knowledgeable mortgage officer who can help you get financing for your real estate purchase or refinance?

**Realtor** Do you have an experienced Realtor who can help you buy or sell and get the best price and terms on your next real estate transaction?

---

### Kristie Smith – Realtor: "Buying AND Selling"

"The home-buying and selling process is a major event that takes lots and lots of vendors and resources to make happen. I recently had a client who not only sold a house, but bought a new home here locally, as well. So, not only did they need to sell their home, there was a lot to do to get it ready for sale. They had some wood rot on the outside of their home that I knew was going to be an inspection issue and buyers would notice immediately.

So the handyman or the general contractor needed to go in and do a few punch-list items. I always ask people to get their furnace serviced before we put it on the market, because buyers look at the furnace. So we get the HVAC guy in to look at the furnace, we deal with the wood rot, and sometimes the carpets are a mess! We need to either get them cleaned with our carpet cleaner or we need to get my wholesale flooring company to get in there and just replace the carpets.

We also bring in the cleaning service in my networking group with a referral to make the place sparkle and smell good. So the initial listing period for me to get the house ready to go to market creates referrals for a lot of people."

## *Wellness Business Categories*

Wellness Contact Sphere business categories serve a crossover need, helping the person in the Real Estate Key Situation save both time and money with improved energy and overall health.

**Chiropractor**  Do you have a good chiropractor to help ease your aches and pains so you can be at your best while focused on your Real Estate Key Situation?

**Life Coach**  Are you working with an experienced life coach to help set and achieve your goals and stay on track with your plan as you work through your Real Estate Key Situation?

---

*Judith Joyce* *–Journey Beyond Belief – Life Coach:*
*"New Construction Stress Test"*

*"In my experience as a life coach, I've found that building a home can be one of the most stressful situations for a husband and wife to go through together. The basic issue is usually their individual styles and the way they communicate and get together to make decisions. It can be overwhelming with the massive number of decisions, both large and small. From keeping an eye on the builder during the construction, watching the details of the workmanship, as well as whether or not things are done on schedule and within the budget, to the design, finish materials, landscaping, and a lot more, it can be very difficult.*

*A good life coach will support how they make decisions, help them to compromise and work together to keep the common goal in mind, which is not only to build a great house, but to keep a happy marriage!"*

**Massage**  Have you thought of working with a massage therapist to reward yourself, increase efficiency and improve your feeling of well being so you can focus on your Real Estate Key Situation?

**Nutrition**  Are you taking the best nutritional products to help you maintain optimal brain function and increase stamina while focused on your Real Estate Key situation?

**Personal Trainer**  Do you know a personal trainer you can trust to help you keep your energy level up and stay in great shape while working through your Real Estate Key Situation?

**Water Purification**  Do you know a water quality professional to make sure you and the occupants of your property are drinking, cooking and bathing in healthy water?

# Afterword

At the end of the day, this book is all about "opportunity recognition." Now that you've looked at business networking and referral marketing from a wide variety of different angles and alternate perspectives, do you see money on the table you've been overlooking?

We're betting you do!

Apply the lessons you've learned from the Six Key Situations to form a Power Team around your own targeted prospects, Key Situations and favorable referral circumstances.

We would love to hear your success stories and networking secrets – email us at abe@moneyonthetablebook.com

For additional resources including free downloads of all Money on the Table forms and flyers visit www.moneyonthetablebook.com

*"May the only money you leave on the table be a generous tip for excellent service!"*

# About the Authors

**Dr. Ivan Misner** is the Founder and Chairman of BNI, the world's largest business networking organization. BNI was founded in 1985 and the organization now has thousands of groups throughout every populated continent of the world. Each year, BNI generates millions of referrals resulting in billions of dollars worth of business for its members.

Ivan's Ph.D. is from the University of Southern California. He has written 14 books, including three *New York Times* bestsellers, as well as his recent bestseller, **Networking Like a Pro**. He is a monthly columnist for Entrepreneur.com and is the Senior Partner for the Referral Institute, a referral training company with trainers around the world. In addition, he has taught business management and social capital courses at several universities throughout the United States.

Called "The Father of Modern Networking" by CNN and "The Networking Guru" by Entrepreneur magazine, Ivan is considered to be one of the world's leading experts on business networking and has been a keynote speaker for major corporations and associations throughout the world. He has been featured in the Los Angeles Times, Wall Street Journal, and New York Times, as well as numerous TV and radio shows on CNN, CNBC, and the BBC in London.

Ivan is on the Board of Trustees for the University of LaVerne. He is also the Founder of the BNI-Misner Charitable Foundation and was recently named Humanitarian of the Year by a southern California newspaper. He is married and lives with his wife, Elisabeth, and their three children in Claremont, California. In his spare time (!!!), he is also an amateur magician and a black belt in karate.

**Lee Abraham** is the author of *The Art of Business Networking*, founder of FAST180 Press, and Senior Vice President of Consulting for MaxAvenue, an intellectual property and consulting firm specializing in real estate.

A veteran of 30+ years in the real estate industry, Lee has a wealth of personal experience as a broker, salesman, appraiser, expert witness and investor, as well as being the owner of a home inspection business. Also a seasoned networker and trainer, Lee has been a member of BNI for 20 years, currently serving as an Area Director for BNI in Northern Arizona.

With MaxAvenue, Lee combines his passion for training business professionals to achieve their goals through structured referral networking with his wide ranging real estate expertise and deep appreciation of MaxAvenue's Lifetime Value Business Model™.

As founder of FAST180 Press, Lee enjoys making his books available for co-author and private label printing to businesses, groups and organizations in all industries for branding, marketing and promotional campaigns, as well as word-of-mouth referral training programs. For more information visit www. fast180.com

Lee and his wife Marcía live in Prescott Valley, Arizona, and inspired by their three adult children, Rachel, Joe, and David, are currently working on their first book together, *The Art of Friendship*.

# Appendix

## Ten Key Questions Worksheet

**Money on the Table
Ten Key Questions Worksheet**

1) How did you get started in your business?

2) What do you enjoy most about what you do? Can you tell me about a recent client that you really enjoyed helping?

3) What separates you and/or your company from the competition?

4) What advice would you give someone starting out in your business?

5) What are the coming trends in your business or industry?

6) What strategies have you found to be the most effective in promoting your business?

7) If there was anything about your business or industry that you could change what would it be?

8) What is the next big event coming up for you?

9) What is your biggest challenge at the moment?

10) What type of customers are you looking for? How will I recognize a good prospect for you? Which Lifecycle Events are your targeted prospects experiencing?

# Connector to Creator Worksheet

These are the Six Key Situations. Select the three you feel are most appropriate to your business.

☐ BUSINESS BUILDER  ☐ RELOCATION
☐ GETTING HEALTHY  ☐ NEW BABY
☐ GETTING MARRIED  ☐ REAL ESTATE

Last Name / First Name _____
Telephone Number: _____
Business Category: _____
Scope of Products & Services: _____

| KEY SITUATION | Key Situation 1: | Key Situation 2: | Key Situation 3: | Custom Key Situation 1: | Custom Key Situation 2: | Custom Key Situation 3: |
|---|---|---|---|---|---|---|
| GOLDEN GOOSE: | | | | | | |
| BRAG ABOUT: | | | | | | |
| | My _____ is someone I like and trust as a person because: | | Everyone I talk to who has worked with my _____ says: | | | |
| LISTEN and LOOK FOR: | | | | | | |

# Power Team Action Grid

## Power Team Action Grid

**Power Team Partners:**

**Business Category:**

### RESEARCH / PREPARATION

**INSTRUCTIONS:** Enter completion date for each activity listed below

- Complete 10 Key Questions
- Key Situations/Targeted Prospects
- Golden Goose Referrals
- Brag About
- Look/Listen

### PROMOTIONAL ACTIVITY

**INSTRUCTIONS:** Enter completion date for each activity listed below

- To Clients
- To Co-Workers
- At Business Events
- To Potential Golden Geese

### GROUP ACTIVITY

**INSTRUCTIONS:** Enter completion date for each activity listed below

- Display Business Cards
- Websites, Links & Reviews
- Combine Advertising
- Combine Efforts at Trade Shows
- Create Custom Key Situations
- Schedule a Job Tour
- Host a Workshop or Seminar
- Host a Social Event

### REFERRAL TRACKING

**INSTRUCTIONS:** Enter completion date for each activity listed below

- Given/Received Inside Referrals
- Given/Received Outside Referrals
- Created a Golden Goose

# Power Team Report Card

## Power Team Report Card

| Do I..? | REGULARLY | SOMETIMES | RARELY |
|---|---|---|---|
| Arrive early or on time for my networking group meetings | | | |
| Introduce myself to visitors at the meetings | | | |
| Prepare my Sales Force Update in advance | | | |
| Alternate the Targeted Prospects I train my Power Team to recognize | | | |
| Meet individually with other Power Team members | | | |
| Successfully train Power Team members to give compelling testimonials | | | |
| Diligently seek Bragging Buddy opportunities for my Power Team | | | |
| Carry a stocked and current business card organizer | | | |
| Give high quality referrals to meet or exceed group standards | | | |
| Invite potential networking partners to meet with the Power Team leader | | | |
| Follow up quickly on referrals I receive | | | |
| Keep referral sources updated on follow up activity | | | |
| Exceed client expectations and consistently make referral sources look good | | | |
| Thank people who give me referrals | | | |
| Keep the Power Team up to date with my current marketing tools | | | |
| Dress to meet or exceed expectations | | | |
| Maintain an enthusiastic and positive attitude | | | |
| Engage in Open Networking Opportunities | | | |
| Invest time in personal development & communication skills | | | |
| Invest time in professional development & communication skills | | | |
| Total | | | |
| Scores | x5 | x3 | x1 |
| TOTAL SCORE | | | |

**Scoring System**
95+ Power Team Hall of Famer
85+ Power Team All Star
70+ Power Team Role Player
60+ Power Team Bench Warmer

# GAINS Profile

## GAINS Worksheet

**GOALS**

**Goals**  Goals are the business or personal objectives you want or need to meet for yourself or the people who are important to you. You need to define your goals and have a clear picture of the other person's goals. The best way to build a relationship with someone is to help them achieve their goals!

**ACCOMPLISHMENTS**

**Accomplishments**  People like to talk about the things they are proud of. Remember, some of your best insight into others comes from knowing what goals they have already achieved. Your knowledge, skills, experiences and values can be surmised from your achievements. Be ready to share your accomplishments with the people you meet.

**INTERESTS**

**Interests**  Your interests can help you connect with others. Interests are things like playing sports, reading books and listening to music. People like to spend time with those who share their interests. When you and your network source share the same interests, it will strengthen your relationship.

**NETWORKS**

**Networks**  You have many networks, both formal and informal. A network can be an organization, institution, company or individual you associate with.

**SKILLS**

**Skills**  The more you know about the talents and abilities of the people in your network, the better equipped you are to find (and refer) competent, affordable products and services when the need arises. And when you're trying to round up business opportunities, the more people you know about your skills, the better your chances!

★ How well do you know the people you want to include in your network? Chances are you have a little homework to do. Spend more time with the people you already know and concentrate on learning these five essentials-their goals, accomplishments, interests, networks, and skills. Make sure you give back the same kind of information. The more they know about you, the faster your name will come to mind when an opportunity arises in which your products, services, knowledge, skills or experience might play a part.

# GAINS Profile Quiz: (Page 1 of 2)

## Quiz Facts You Should Know about Each Member of Your Network

Select a Network Member with whom you are familiar and supply the following information about him or her. Try to complete the quiz within 15 minutes without help. Use your memory and any personal or professional resource at your disposal, such as directories, card files, notes and online data. If the correct response is "none" or "not applicable," write "none." If you don't know the answer, leave it blank. Score 4 points for each complete, correct answer, 2 points for each partial answer. Highest possible score: 100 points. This exercise is most valuable if you discuss the answers with the individual after you finish.

Name_____

### Personal Information:                                                                      Points

A. Nickname                                                                                    _____

B: Date and place of birth                                                                     _____

C: A favorite color or food                                                                    _____

D: Best friend (other than yourself)                                                           _____

E: Mentor/sponsor/role model/hero (other than yourself)                                        _____

F: Favorite TV program, song or hobby                                                          _____

G: A personal award or recognition                                                             _____

H: Type of pet or vehicle                                                                      _____

Answer either the Employment or the Business/Enterprise section below:

### Employment:                                                                                Points

I: Name and location of current place of employment                                            _____

J: Job title and at least one major duty                                                       _____

K: Name and title of current boss                                                              _____

L: Name of one co-worker                                                                       _____

M: A work-related award achievement                                                            _____

N: Career objective or plan                                                                    _____

O: Name and location of another company he or she has worked for                               _____

## Business/Enterprise:                                              Points

I.  Name and location of business                                    _____

J.  Name, key benefits, features, and price of one product or service   _____

K.  One type of individual or group in target market                 _____

L.  Major business issue/objective/problem                           _____

M.  Reason he or she decided to enter this business                  _____

N.  Number of years in this business or industry                     _____

O.  Name of a vendor, staff member, or client                        _____

## Memberships:                                                      Points

P:  One or more of the community groups, clubs, or organizations he or she has belonged to, office or position held, and name of at least one other member   _____

Q.  One or more of the business associations or groups he or she has belonged to, office or position held, and name of at least one other member   _____

## Residence and Family:                                             Points

R.  City of Residence                                                _____

S.  Home Phone Number                                                _____

T.  Name, occupation of spouse/significant other                     _____

U.  No. children or siblings (and at least one name)                 _____

V  parent's or guardian's name and occupation                        _____

## Education:                                                        Points

W.  Name at least one school attended (high school, college, vocational, etc.)   _____

X.  Certificate, degree, credentials, license or special training received   _____

Y.  Newspaper, magazine, news letter, other publication read regularly, or other publication read regularly for educational or information about events and opportunities   _____

### Total Points     _____

*BNI, the world's largest business networking organization, was founded by Dr. Ivan Misner in 1985, as a way for businesspeople to generate referrals in a structured, professional environment. The organization, now the world's largest referral business network, has thousands of chapters with tens of thousands of members on every populated continent. Since the organization's inception, BNI members have passed millions of referrals, generating billions of dollars in business for the participants.*

*The primary purpose of the organization is to pass qualified business referrals to its members. The philosophy of BNI can be summed up in two simple words: Givers Gain®. If you give business to people, you will get business from them. BNI allows only one person per profession to join a chapter. The program is designed to help business people develop long-term relationships, thereby creating a basis for trust and inevitably, referrals. The mission of BNI is to help members increase their business through a structured, positive, and professional word-of-mouth program that enables them to develop long-term, meaningful relationships with quality business professionals.*

*To visit a chapter near you, contact BNI via e-mail at bni@bni.com or visit its website at bni.com.*

# REFERRAL™ INSTITUTE

The Referral Institute is a leading referral training organization, with franchises, trainers, and coaches around the world. The organization teaches business professionals how to harness the power of referral marketing to drive sales for long-term, sustainable business growth by referral. Founded in 2001, the Referral Institute began developing training materials specific to referral marketing and was recently recognized by Entrepreneur.com as one of the top 500 franchised companies in the world.

The Referral Institute's mission is to help people create Referrals for Life®. In total, the Referral Institute provides the world's leading material on referral marketing.

The organization offers students one-day programs, as well as courses covering several modules over 10 to 12 weeks. The Pipeline Program, the organization's signature class, requires participants to attend the class with a referral source. The one-day Pipeline Seminar teaches a simple, highly manageable referral process by which participants leave the training having already scheduled appointments with qualified prospects.

The Referral Institute's 10 to 12 week course is called Certified Networker®. This course is truly a foundation for understanding, developing, and tracking your referral business. In most cases, Certified Networker simply changes the way business owners do business. It narrows their target market, provides them with mission statements, and shows them how profitable it can be to develop referral sources by being strategic. Certified Networker is a must for anyone new to referral marketing.

Please go to referralinstitute.com to learn more about referral marketing as well as how to attend a Referral Institute training program in your area. You may contact the organization at info@referralinstitute.com to talk about growing your business by generating qualified referrals.

The BNI-Misner Foundation is a non-profit program that supports charitable causes relating to children and education in countries where BNI is operating. The primary focus of the foundation is to provide small mini-grants for educational projects.

A portion of the proceeds from this book have been donated to support the BNI-Misner Foundation's good work!

Go to *www.BNIfoundation.org* to learn more.

**Experts write books!** Need help writing yours? FAST180 Press specializes in co-authored books and transforming business experts into published authors.

*"Being the author of a published book is one of the most powerful ways to increase credibility as an expert. However, there are many people with legitimate expertise who do not have the time, resources or necessary writing skills to become published authors; this 'co-author' opportunity from Lee Abraham and FAST180 Press is the ultimate solution!"*

**Dr. Ivan Misner, NY Times Bestselling author and Founder of BNI and Referral Institute**

Private label and bulk purchase books for businesses, groups and organizations are also available for branding opportunities, promotional use and training programs.

For more information, please contact
# Lee Abraham
FAST180 Press
(928) 713-1563
abe@moneyonthetablebook.com
Fast180.com
Moneyonthetablebook.com
Blog: http://fast180.wordpress.com/
Follow Lee on Twitter: http://twitter.com/fast180

# Index

Testimonial  47, 53, 56, 61, 62, 63, 67, 69, 71, 73, 83, 87, 109, 110, 113, 114, 117, 118, 120, 123, 125, 150, 151, 154, 170, 182

Testimonials  47, 53, 56, 61, 62, 63, 67, 69, 71, 73, 83, 87, 109, 110, 113, 114, 117, 118, 120, 123, 125, 150, 151, 154, 170, 182

Time Confidence Curve  47, 53, 56, 61, 62, 63, 67, 69, 71, 73, 83, 87, 109, 110, 113, 114, 117, 118, 120, 123, 125, 150, 151, 154, 170, 182

Trigger Questions  47, 53, 56, 61, 62, 63, 67, 69, 71, 73, 83, 87, 109, 110, 113, 114, 117, 118, 120, 123, 125, 150, 151, 154, 170, 182

Twitter  47, 53, 56, 61, 62, 63, 67, 69, 71, 73, 83, 87, 109, 110, 113, 114, 117, 118, 120, 123, 125, 150, 151, 154, 170, 182

## V

VCP
  VCP Process  47, 53, 56, 61, 62, 63, 67, 69, 71, 73, 83, 87, 109, 110, 113, 114, 117, 118, 120, 123, 125, 150, 151, 154, 170, 182
Visibility  45, 51, 52, 91, 92, 94, 95, 99, 100, 102, 103

## W

Walker, Hazel  40, 88, 100, 119, 120, 162
Word-of-mouth  47, 53, 56, 61, 62, 63, 67, 69, 71, 73, 83, 87, 109, 110, 113, 114, 117, 118, 120, 123, 125, 150, 151, 154, 170, 182

## Z

Zanoff, Joel  176, 187, 196, 208, 219